The Art of
ADAPTIVE
COMMUNICATION

The Art of
ADAPTIVE
COMMUNICATION

BUILD POSITIVE PERSONAL CONNECTIONS WITH ANYONE

Kahler Communications, Inc.

Rev. date: 09/06/2017

To order additional copies of this book, contact:
Xlibris
1-888-795-4274
www.Xlibris.com
Orders@Xlibris.com
764034

CONTENTS

PART I

The Basics of the Process Communication Model®

PART 2

Applying The Process Communication Model Concepts

If you look for wood, you will find wood.
If you look for love, you will find love.
If you look for hate, you will find hate.
A Tuareg proverb
To Antéo

ACKNOWLEDGMENTS

I am grateful to Dr. Taibi Kahler, Ph.D., for his confidence and friendship.

I am grateful to Robert S. Wert, Phyllis Baltz, David Kaiser, Heather Cuccias, Jérôme Lefeuvre and Cyril Collignon for their benevolent vigilance and precious contribution to this English version.

PREFACE

The Process Communication Model® has been evolving for over thirty-five years. The tool's development dates back to when I was studying at Purdue. At the time, I was an intern at a local psychiatric hospital. In observing our patients, I noticed that, just before exhibiting clearly inappropriate behavior, they used gestures, body language and facial expressions that formed a very specific and unique set for diagnosis.

One of the clinical models I was studying at the time, Transactional Analysis, was suitable for interpreting these observations. Just before someone shows behavior such as "I'm OK, you're not OK" or "I'm not OK, you're OK", they use the same range of behaviors (words, tone, gestures, body language and facial expression).

The work I conducted based on these observations resulted in the identification and classification of five groups of behaviors that I called Be Perfect, Try Hard, Be Strong, Please and Hurry up. I called these behaviors "drivers" since they appeared to "drive" subjects into deeper distress. This initial research revealed significant correlations that are particularly useful in predicting negative behavior in distress situations. I called these sequences, "miniscripts".

A few years later, this work received the Eric Berne Memorial Scientific Award, discerned by ten thousand of my peers.

I subsequently became interested in the positive, as well as the negative aspects of the personality. Out of concern for transparency, I translated the technical and clinical terms describing communication and miscommunication into everyday language.

In 1978, Dr. Terry McGuire, the psychiatrist in charge of recruiting and training astronauts for NASA, asked me to assist him. With the aim of facilitating and standardizing the selection process, I validated a questionnaire based on the following points: personality structure, personality types (Thinker, Harmonizer, Rebel, Imaginer, Promoter, Persister), character strengths, personality parts communication channels, perceptions, preferred environments, management styles, control range, psychological motivators and personal and professional distress sequences and patterns.

During this validation study, I began to understand the importance of the significant correlations between psychological needs and personality types, typical failure mechanisms and unresolved issues. If an individual cannot satisfy his or her psychological needs positively, that person continues to display the same distress sequences in an attempt to satisfy these needs, only negatively. This is the key to predictable behavior. Furthermore, sustained distress behavior is often correlated to an unresolved issue. Resolving that issue results in "phasing" into another part of one's personality structure. This change in phase in turn causes the appearance of a new psychological need and therefore a new source of motivation.

Currently, over one million two hundred thousand people have experienced the Process Communication Model – whether in a business or personal context. Current research in different universities aims to use the model in large companies as well as applications in schools and families.

The Process Communication Model is a precious tool for understanding and appreciating ourselves and others and is now available across 46 countries in 22 languages.

I was fortunate to have worked with some highly competent, talented, loyal people to whom I can pass the torch. One of those people and a friend, Gérard Collignon, whose book you are about to read sheds light on new horizons for using the Process Communication Model. His style is bright, fresh, open and straightforward. He helps the reader discover this model by giving true-life examples and makes the process lively by inviting the reader to share the everyday lives of six personality types. It is both a documentary and a novel, a statistical report and a handbook on how to improve the quality of life for one's self, and for one's family, friends and coworkers.

Out of all of the pearls of wisdom and wonderful insight on human nature and the dynamics of the personality that Eric Berne gave us in his many writings, I am particularly fond of this one: a theory is never complete until we are able to translate it into the language of an eight year-old. Personally, if I may add something, I would say that a model is never complete until it can be used by an eight year-old.

Gérard Collignon has achieved this level of simplicity and application. Our future is not only based on our understanding of ourselves; we must also know how to communicate and show others who we are and what we are. This is particularly true for our children, who should get off to the best start possible. Knowledge is essential, wisdom is indispensable. Thank you Gérard.

Taibi Kahler, Ph.D.
Little Rock, Arkansas

INTRODUCTION

"We are continually touched and questioned by communication. In order to understand one's self, we need to be understood by others; to be understood by others, we need to understand others."[i]

Thomas Hora

Author – Our world has become exponentially complex and fast-paced. That is why effective communication is so critically important. We all can relate to that apparent simple email that was sent out that resulted in so much drama, distress, and negative energy. The critical key of effective communication is learning the skill to be able to adapt to each individual and environments such that we "Understand to be Understood"…

Joan: Psst…

Author: Yes?

Joan: That sounds a tad overblown…

Author: Okay… (*sigh*) I'll start over. Between the custodian and the CEO, the politician and his children, a spouse and a mother-in-law, there are many factors involved in communication and many traps to avoid. Whether it be for managerial or commercial purposes, political or advertising purposes, or family or friendly purposes, sooner or later, everyone wants to hear or transmit a message. In other words, to be on the same wave length as the person we're talking to. Is that better?

Joan: Well, yeah.

Author: One of the main obstacles in transmitting an effective message is that we hope, even expect, that others will react like us, in a way we find acceptable, when, ultimately, we are not all "wired" the same way. Understanding the different kinds of "wiring" in each individual and thereby adapting the message specifically to the individual increases the effectiveness of our communication dramatically.

Joan: Awesome!

Author: Shh! As I was saying… In the 1970's, an American psychologist named Dr. Taibi Kahler, practicing in the field of Transactional Analysis, observed that in every patient there was a predictable sequence of negative behaviors, starting with defensive behavior, next moving to more significant distressed outbursts or self-victimization and ending with depressed behavior. This discovery, for which he earned the Eric Berne Memorial Scientific award for 1977, was called the miniscript. With this, Dr. Kahler answered a remark by Eric Berne some years earlier: "The clinician who can figure out how to identify a patient's script in one session will make a capital contribution in terms of our knowledge of humans and how they function psychologically."

Dr. Kahler realized the greater effectiveness of supporting people by stressing the positive aspects of their personality rather than just focusing on their negative behaviors. By furthering the works by Shapiro[ii], he began researching positive characteristics that correlated to the miniscripts that he had discovered. Through his research, he found that they indeed correlate. The totality of Dr. Kahler's research resulted in the *Personality Types* on which Process Communication Model® is based. There are six of them, each with its strong points and weak points. Every person possess all six of the Personality Types within his or her Personality Structure and can access and express the characteristics of each of them, but one of them is dominant.

Learning the characteristics of the Personality Types provides three essential pieces of information: each individual's main source of motivation, their preferred communication mode, and their very personal way of managing stress.

Jack: How can we know a person's source of motivation?

Author: A series of specific "Psychological Needs" corresponds to each Personality Type. And each person systematically seeks to satisfy those needs, resulting in very predictable behaviors. If a person does not obtain positive satisfaction of these needs, they will try to satisfy them in a negative way, resulting in ineffective, even harmful, behavior in both their personal and professional lives without being aware of it. *The positive satisfaction of these Psychological Needs is a person's primary motivation.* The negative satisfaction of these needs is a person's predictable distress behavior.

Each Personality Type also uses a preferential Communication Channel. The *Communication Channel* represents the wave length on which two people can effectively communicate. The Process Communication Model defines five Communication Channels. Knowing them and how to use them helps ensure the quality and effectiveness of your communication. As demonstrated by researchers from the Palo Alto school, "we cannot not communicate".[iii] On the other hand, when we try to communicate outside of the correct Communication Channels, we will miscommunicate.

Jack: How do you define the "distress sequences"?

Author: The level of distress is usually related to the quality of communication and the satisfaction of a person's most important Psychological Needs. Taibi Kahler identified three "degrees" of distress that represent successively greater degrees of *miscommunication*. At the first degree of distress, miscommunication is beginning, most often because someone is trying to communicate with us without using our preferred Channel of Communication and Perception. At the second degree of distress, we exhibit *failure mechanisms*. We are not necessarily aware of these behaviors and they can cause serious problems in both our personal and professional lives. For instance, a manager who notes that "nothing's going right" will start to *crusade*, wielding the carrot and the stick, flip-flopping between threats and sermons which invites others to exhibit their own failure patters, such as *over-adaptation* or *rebellion*. A dad who is totally absorbed by his business life becomes unavailable to his children, a husband becomes rigid about the household budget or vacation, a child refuses schoolwork, etc...

The third degree of distress is fortunately quite rare. It usually manifests as a state of deep crisis, depression, burn-out, despair or even suicidal behavior.

Taibi Kahler discovered the phenomenon of Phase changing, shedding particularly relevant light on individual dynamics and giving us a better understanding of a person's potential *life path* and the origin of our choices and major decisions.

Each person has a Personality Structure composed of all six Personality Types, but one of them is dominant and known as the "Base". The person uses the aspects of the other types less often and less naturally unless he or she has experienced a Phase change or *Phasing*. When Phasing occurs, the person's most urgent Psychological Needs and motivations, together with his or her primary Distress Sequence, changes to those associated with the Personality Type on the next floor of their Personality Structure. However, the person's preferred Perception, Personality Part, and Channel of Communication remains those associated with his or her Base type. This concept helps identify the spontaneous, long-lasting changes that occur in a person and follow the corresponding change in that person's sources of motivation. He designed the Process Communication Model as a model that enables us to anticipate the new sources of motivation and also the behavior an individual may develop in the future, by observing the opportunities for changing Phases presented in their Personality Structure.

Jack: Who has used the concepts of the Process Communication Model?

Author: NASA's Lead Psychiatrist for Manned Space Flight, Dr. Terrence McGuire, worked with Taibi Kahler to use his ideas in the selection and training of astronauts for almost twenty years. The concepts were used to evaluate the compatibility of the teams and predict their behavior once they were confined in a space capsule somewhere in outer space. Under such extreme conditions, it was a good idea to put people together whose psychological profiles had been carefully studied and whose ability to communicate and behavior under stress had been evaluated. Taibi Kahler and his team developed a method that was able to predict the type of reaction astronauts would have in situations of light and severe distress.

The Process Communication Model proposes a *communication philosophy*. One of its primary benefits is providing a true understanding of another's behavior instead of a negative interpretation. Instead of interpreting someone as "lazy" or "an idiot", the model provides insight regarding the actual reasons underlying the behavior – very often Personality Type specific distress behavior. This helps us be in an "I'm ok/you're ok" or "+/+" position. In this position each person recognizes his or her own value and that of the other person. The Process Communication Model facilitates our being in a +/+ position because it provides us with simple signs for understanding miscommunication situations. Many relational problems arise from situations in which the speakers do not understand one another and, instead, project their own interpretation – the one that fits their unique Perception - on the other person's behavior. In business, this misinterpretation system often is reinforced by corporate culture.

The model is simple, but it is not a tool that can be used effectively without being integrated. Successful use of the model comes from a real change in the individual and a decision to become more flexible and increase his or her adaptability. The first step in this change is understanding one's self and the building blocks of one's own personality. A tool for helping to achieve this is the Personality Pattern Inventory (the "PPI"), a questionnaire designed by Taibi Kahler to discover the order and strength of each Personality Type in a person's Personality Structure. Once completed and analyzed, the PPI results are used to create profiles and other outputs that describe the various aspects of the person's personality, including their strongest Perceptions, Channels of Communication, Psychological Needs, Distress Sequences, and ways of avoiding or alleviating stress.

Joan: So then, what about the book?

Author: The following pages first meet a practical objective. They present the individual in all of his or her personal or professional dimensions, in everything that makes up his or her psychological and social life. Many aspects are addressed using concrete cases to help readers better understand and recognize themselves. In the first section of the book, the model's basics are presented: Personality Types, Personality Structure and Phase changes, Channels of Communication, Psychological Needs, miscommunication, and distress. The second section proposes a number of applications for the model, in particular in the fields of management, team cohesion, and sales, as well as in personal life. Each chapter is designed so that readers may refer to them based on their interests, independently of the other parts. This book is also a chance to get to know six people: Isabelle, who has a Harmonizer Base; Jack, who has a Thinker Base; Joan, with a Rebel Base; Peter, who has a Persister Base; Anne, with an Imaginer Base; and Tom, with a Promoter Base. They illustrate the six Personality Types who all work for the same company, Sofia's & Co., and who have also all decided to learn and use Process Communication Model.

PART I

The Basics of the Process Communication Model®

CHAPTER 1

PERSONALITY TYPES

> "It's 12:45 on the big drive south to the beach. At a roadside diner, a few tables away, a smiling, relaxed, thirty-something mom is with her two daughters. The girls resemble one another to a tee; they are dressed alike and apparently are identical twins.
>
> We observe their interaction with amusement and fascination. One of them is running from table to table, looking for customers who are willing to play with her. Meanwhile, the other one stays close to her mom. She likes to cuddle, never leaves the table, and doesn't seek her sister's company or play. The first of the two little girls is exhibiting the behavior of the "Rebel" type, the second one's behavior corresponds to that of the "Harmonizer" type.

The qualifiers "Rebel" and "Harmonizer" refer to two of the six personality types identified by Dr. Taibi Kahler: Harmonizer, Thinker, Rebel, Promoter, Persister, and Imaginer[1] (the Process Communication Model "Personality Types"). Everyone of us possesses the characteristics of all six of these Personality Types but to different degrees. One of these Types is the most predominant and strongest that is unique to each person and is called the "Base Personality Type" or "Base". This

---

[1] The terms used to designate the different Personality Types are not meant to reflect any of negative connotations sometimes attributed to them. See portraits below.

helps us to understand why we share certain key traits with other people, while still being unique.

Each Personality Type has a series of unique attributes:

- Behavioral characteristics (attire, environmental style, character strengths, etc.).
- A key mode of perceiving the world around them. (a "Perception")
- One or two psychological needs whose satisfaction determines each person's unique motivation and positive energy and, on the flip side, that individual's very personal and predictable way of exhibiting distress.
- A preferred "Communication Channel" that helps find the right "frequency" on which to communicate.

No one type is better or worse than another. They all have their strengths and weaknesses and the Process Communication Model does not involve any form of value judgement. It enables each of us to:

- The ability to assess the different facets of our own behavior and those we interact with.
- The ability to genuinely connect with others through understanding of how each person uniquely communicates thereby increasing the quality of our communication.
- Understanding what motivates us and those we interact with. You will learn the skills how to "decode" human behavior through active observation such that you will know what unique motivational needs are desired not only for ourselves but also for those around us.
- Resolve conflict through understanding the predictable and unique distress patterns of ourselves and those around us. These predictable negative behaviors can sabotage us and others both personally and professionally. You will learn what are the underlying causes of these negative behaviors and strategies to invite others out of distress.

The Process Communication Model has been used in businesses for over thirty years and it has been shown to be applicable across all races, cultures, and languages. In North America the Harmonizer type is the most prevalent, followed by Thinker, Rebel, Persister, Imaginer, and Promoter. Data from outside of the North America has indicated similar results.

HARMONIZER TYPE[2]

- Isabelle, do you want to come to gym class?
- No...
- That's odd, you were so happy to be getting some exercise...
- Yeah, I don't know why I don't feel like going. Maybe's it's the place: that gloomy, unheated, old schoolroom and the teacher never smiles. It's as if she doesn't care about anyone. I feel like finding a warmer place, closer to home, which would allow me more time with my family in the evening. I really don't feel up to going today. I'd rather have a hot bath and a cup of tea.

We could continue to talk with Isabelle. She would easily tell us about what personally concerns her. With her Harmonizer Base, she attaches a lot of importance to sensations and the quality of human relations. Her "big-hearted" side and concern for the views others have of her would have an important place in our discussion.

Isabelle perceives the world through the filter of her emotions – her primary Perception. She integrates things and people through feelings. One of her key personality traits: she loves to be loved...

But isn't that the case with everyone? Definitely and we can distinguish certain differences as everyone has a preferred primary Perception: some people prefer to be loved for their ideas, or for their charm, or acts of bravery, or they want their accomplishments to be recognized.

For Isabelle, being unconditionaly loved for being herself is what counts. So she tries to give the same signs of recognition to others that she needs.

Unconditional love? It's the meaning of life.

Her physical appearance is well-groomed. She often wears attractively matched pastels. She likes jewelry and regularly goes to the

---

[2] Each of these examples is of someone who is almost "purely" of the Type described. In reality, we all have all six Types within us and we generally are capable of accessing the other Types and exhibiting their characteristics.

hairdresser: showing up at a meeting sloppily dressed or without her make-up is out of the question.

Certain objects are also very important in Isabelle's life. They are chosen as souvenirs of an emotional history and used to create an inviting atmosphere. Her desk, for example, holds a few family photos, potted plants, and other reminders that life is not entirely about files. In other words, "priority to people".

Her environment is usually comfortable in a "cozy nest" style. At home, soft music and discreet fragrances are also a feature. She knows how to create harmony and is attentive to other people's needs. Adjectives like compassionate, sensitive, and warm describe her perfectly. Those are the Process Communication Model "Character Strengths" uniquely associated with the Harmonizer. During a seminar break, she is often the one to spontaneously serve drinks to the other members of the group, the interests of others always taking priority over her own. In fact, she sometimes has trouble affirming herself, or "taking her place". When this happens, she seems to lack self-assurance and her speech will contain phrases like "maybe" and "if I'm not mistaken", expressed in a soft, high-pitched voice. One of her key difficulties is recognizing her limits and saying no as she seeks to please others. Her staff often thinks she overdoes it and lets herself be overrun by too much solicitation.

She tends to look younger than her age, even if her face is marked with charming expression lines. The ones from worry can sometimes take the shape of half-circles over her eyes (she tends to raise her eyebrows). Since her existential question is "Am I loveable?" her most severe distress will come from the end of a significant emotional relationship.

She needs to "feel good" at work, ideally with a warmhearted boss and belonging to a team with a pleasant working atmosphere. Under stress, Isabelle tends to discredit herself, to think that it's all her fault and makes involuntary "stupid" mistakes. She sometimes also compensates with food: she's a regular dieter... on penance days.

Her best source of renewal and motivation: positive recognition of her as a person, not her performance, a pleasant environment in terms of the senses (a cozy "homey" restaurant, sauna, massage). Her ideal apartment? She can see it equipped with a winter garden, sunny bay windows and... Harmonizer neighbors.

About 30% of the North American population has a Harmonizer Base, three-quarters of whom are female and one-quarter male.

These naturally compassionate communicators often work in helping occupations: doctors, social workers (professions they share with the Persister type), nurses, psychotherapists, or else as flight attendants, receptionists, PR agents, waiters and waitresses, etc. Some examples of a Harmonizer Base are: Mister Rogers, Dinah Shore, and Mother Theresa.

Table 1.1: Characteristics of the Harmonizer Type

Character Strengths	Compassionate, sensitive, warm.
Characteristics	The ability to be "giving", attentive to others' needs. Good at creating harmony.
Expressing feelings	Easily. Uses them to communicate.
Appearance	Well-groomed. Soft, matching colors.
Preferred business fields	Communication. Public Relations. Helping professions. Service occupations.
Environment	Warm, welcoming, comfortable, personalized, both at home and at the office.
Perception	Emotions. Feels first. Perceives people and situations through feelings towards them.
Team behavior	Strives to build and encourage cooperative relationships.
Psychological needs	Recognition as a person. A nourishing environment for the senses.

THINKER TYPE

When Isabelle arrived at the office this morning, she ran into Jack in the hallway: three files under his arm, forehead creased with a pronounced horizontal worry line… In other words, he looked like he had started his day much earlier. In fact, it is not rare for Jack to start early and finish later than everyone else. It's as if he just can't stop until he has finished all work in front of him. But, since it's never-ending…

Isabelle – Hi Jack! How are you? You look a little tired to me.

Jack – No, no, but I've got a lot to do. We should see each other about organizing the day on the 26th. I need a clear, detailed review. I propose this morning... between 11:45 and 12:30. Unless we do it during lunch hour...

Isabelle – Um... I'd feel better with the first solution. Can I buy you coffee?

Jack – No, thanks. I don't have time. And I find that cafeteria more and more noisy and dirty...

Isabelle goes her way, as usual, slightly bothered by her coworker's responses, "I wonder what it would take to get him to talk about something else other than work."

Jack has a Thinker Base which, for people like Isabelle, can feel like meeting an impersonal computer.

Jack's existential question is "Am I competent?" For that reason, he works hard and devotes his time generously.

He is mainly a serious person. He starts by thinking, looking for facts and information in order to classify them, rank them and draw his conclusions.

Logic is his keyword, organization is his skill, and a sense of responsibility is his daily bread (he often has backaches from its weight).

What we first notice about him is his "clean" look: impeccable, well-groomed, hair perfectly cut. No engaging smiles or joking from him on first contact. He does not spontaneously show human warmth or friendliness and is immediately interested in the facts at hand. He leaves his private life outside the office door and has trouble understanding that this may be different for others. An assistant with a Harmonizer base could quickly find themselves in a desert of non-recognition with a boss like Jack and also feel like they were being treated like a machine. It should be said that, for Jack, getting straight to the point is also synonymous with saving time. Time... is his master. He is the king of planning, at the office, and on vacation. His psychological balance depends on it. In fact, he carefully avoids improvisation and carefully weighs each of his decisions. His annual budget is a masterpiece in that field.

During a TV show on couples and money, a husband with a Thinker Base explained that he felt reassured once he had finished organizing the household budget for the whole year, planning all of the income and all the expenses. On the other hand, his wife who had a Rebel Base, kept spending impulsively and justified it with, "You don't realize it but I got this little dress at 50% off", which naturally caused tension in the couple.

The Thinker's environment often reflects his look: organized and functional. Everything is orderly or else the disorder is carefully structured. Jack can find his way around in it in a fraction of a second. Beware to the cleaner who tries to intervene! Everything has its place and stays there, as if by magic. The furniture style is usually contemporary.

As we have seen, his concerns revolve around competency, organization, and doing a good job. What is most important to him is to be recognized for his thoughts and achievements and for his time to be structured. He uses a lot of energy to satisfy these needs; if they are not satisfied, he becomes distressed. That is when he progressively stops delegating, over-controls, and has more and more difficulty leaving the office. He can show impatience and become rigid on organization and meeting deadlines.

In any case, it is not uncommon for Jack to take work home with him, which his family routinely criticizes him for. Yet, he sincerely believes he is doing everything possible for his loved ones' happiness. With age, worry traces a few horizontal lines across his brow. His greatest risk: forgetting that there is more to life than just work. For Jack, relaxing and doing nothing feels like a waste of time.

If he feels dissatisfied with his business life, if he loses his motivation for various reasons (no longer learning anything, illogical decisions, management inconsistency, etc.), he could invest less in his job. And it is highly probably that he would invest in another part of his social life and get back to functioning like in the good ole days. He might binge on gardening or home improvement. He would only take a few days of vacation because he has to finish the house, keep an eye on the vegetable garden, etc. "Work first, enjoy yourself later", is the motto usually shared by people with a Thinker base. They compose 25% of the U.S. population, three-quarters of whom are males and one-quarter are females. Some examples of a Thinker Base are: Joe Friday from Dragnet, Mr. Spock from Star Trek, and Thomas Pain.

Table 1.2: Characteristics of the Thinker Type

Character Strengths	Logical, responsible, organized.
Characteristics	Analytic. A logical thinker.
Expresses feelings	Rarely. Considered as unnecessary in the working environment.
Appearance	Classic and well-groomed, depending on the situation.
Preferred business fields	Technical. Accounting. Operations. Administration. Tasks requiring organization, method and precision.
Environment	Functional, orderly, contemporary
Perception	Thoughts. Classifies people and things into categories.
Team behavior	Looks for information exchange. Prefers one-on-one relationships over a group.
Psychological needs	Recognition of work. Structured time.

REBEL TYPE

"Yuck! This jitter juice is getting worse and worse," cries Joan with her nose in her coffee cup. She has just entered Jack's office and, noticing him behind the desk, gushes in one breath, "Hey, great tie Dude! Awesome! On the other hand, the circles under your eyes are not quite as decorative..." Jack recoils inwardly, "How can anyone make so much noise in a workplace?" he thinks. "This girl can't stay still. It's not surprising that she always misses her deadlines." Joan settles onto an edge of the table, "Oh, boy," she thinks, "Am I ever going to need this coffee and I'm the one who went to bed at 4 this morning to finish this friggin' script. Okay, where can we get some laughs in here this morning?"

Clearly, Joan has a Rebel Base. Jack tolerates her: he enjoys her sense of humor, she reminds him of his wife but... he can only take her in small doses. Unfortunately, by definition the Rebel type lives outside of predictable norms which they express in various ways: original clothing, flexible hours, and a tendency to look for fun everywhere all the time.

Although she is fundamentally an individualist, Joan needs lots of contact. Playing all by herself does not motivate her. Her playfulness and spontaneous expression makes her the ideal entertainer for a group that she likes to make laugh and enjoys stimulating each person's "inner child". You can count on her to punctuate your meetings with a joke every 10 minutes... She voluntarily lives on the fringes of several groups in which she makes brief, yet appreciated, appearances.

Born creative, she is bubbling with ideas and desires, even if she sometimes has trouble materializing them. She is not motivated by a project's development or management (she would never dream of becoming a CEO). It is important for her to be able to freely express her ideas and feel that her creativity is appreciated. She has difficulty with demands and cannot stand directive or autocratic behavior. However, she doubles her energy whenever someone proposes... that she propose. But as soon as the task becomes monotonous or repetitive, her level of motivation begins to fall off dangerously and it is important for her to plan regular changes of activity.

Posters, bright colors, music, original furniture and objects decorate her office and home. In other words, anything that can satisfy her need for stimulation (she needs "good vibrations", as she says) and her playfulness (in which she is totally invested, since that is where her energy comes from). Her attire is usually designed to attract attention... even negative if need be. "Anything rather than indifference".

Joan perceives people and things by reacting to how she feels: she likes or dislikes, that's it. And anyone who has a problem with that can go fly a kite! She lives in the moment. She has trouble projecting herself into the past or future and, in the event of stress, accepting the consequences of her acts and decisions. If she disagrees with a superior, she can very quickly escalate and push her manager to their limit, at the risk of getting fired. In this case, she tries to find out "just how far she can go", her existential question being "Am I acceptable?"

It goes without saying that Jack sees her as belonging to what some managers call the "unmanageables". It's true that the most spectacular conflicts he has observed at work concerned a Persister Base manager and a Rebel Base employee. In fact, the Rebel type reacts very poorly to obligations, acts out, complains, and very quickly can become unpleasant or blaming. These are the usual signs of distress. Yet, as we will see, managers with a Persister Base do not necessarily have the range of communication that enables them to easily re-establish contact with Rebel type employees. The more the Rebel acts out to get attention, the more her boss will see her behavior as ridiculous and inappropriate. The effective strategy in this case would be to begin by satisfying the employee's need for playful interaction by taking a few seconds to joke before getting down to serious matters.

People with a Rebel Base can usually be found in artistic professions and jobs that require personal creativity. The creative arts such as graphic arts, cinematography, etc...are typically filled with people strong in this Personality Type as it provides them with that creative outlet. They also often have a pronounced taste for leisure activities (vacation hosts, for example). It is estimated that they compose 20% of the North American population, 60% of whom are are female and 25% are male). Some examples of the Rebel Base are: Robin Williams, Thomas Edison, and Hawkeye Pierce from MASH.

Table 1.3 Characteristics of the Rebel Type

Character Strengths	Spontaneous, creative, playful
Characteristics	The ability to play and appreciate the moment: "Carpe Diem"
Expresses feelings	Expresses reactions easily. In the form of spontaneous statements of likes and dislikes
Appearance	Original style
Preferred business fields	Artistic creation, entertainment, tasks requiring creativity
Environment	Fun, full of stimulation, gadgets, etc.
Perception	Reacts to people and things with likes/dislikes
Team behavior	Enjoys the group atmosphere. Does not initiate contact but seizes every opportunity to experience it, especially if it is presented in a playful form.
Psychological needs	Playful contact

PERSISTER TYPE

Peter, who is Isabelle, Jack, and Joan's manager, usually begins conversations with serious subjects. "Oh, brother," murmurs Joan, "when that guy gets an opinion into his head... he's Jack only with convictions...". "And the way he stares me down," notes Isabelle who appreciates Peter's loyalty to his humanist, ethical values that form the company pillars. She calls him "the bighearted bear". She fears his stormy days and his merciless attitude that makes you feel like you've made all the mistakes in the world! It's not enough to disseminate his convictions throughout the firm, Peter also spreads the good word outside. He leads the local community's outreach to help troubled youth.

What is striking about Peter is his gaze: piercing, attentive, it can seem severe. He has a real gift for observation and uses it to evaluate those around him. This attitude isn't always comfortable for others since Peter sets very high standards for both himself and others.

He is a person of commitment in both his business and social life. Many people with a Persister Base feel invested with a mission to which they devote themselves entirely, from transmitting their values to their children (the way they inherited them from their parents), to political activism, and eradicating poverty... Feeling recognized for their opinions and convictions are what motivates them. For the speaker, it is a matter of convincing, for the activist of doing their duty, for the politician of being elected.

Peter's reference is *what he believes*. So he is a pillar of stability for the company whose values he shares, but he can also become a tireless opponent and contradictor. He is known among the team for his persistence. He sets himself a goal and needs to see his projects through. That is why he hates to be interrupted in either his activities or speech (and he likes to give speeches). He shares many points in common with Jack who has a Thinker Base, but while the latter is motivated by the search for facts, Peter first tries to know his contact's opinion or else expresses his own. He interprets the world around him through the Perceptional filter of Opinions. In fact, it is more natural for him to interpret than to analyze.

During a training day, when asked to watch a video and comment on it using a descriptive observation mode, he had a lot of difficulty not interpreting what he saw: "he's doing that for such and such a reason", "he should..." etc.

His weak point? Listening, because his natural motivation is first to be heard. He is often the one who interrupts because he is focusing on his idea and not listening to the other person. In a seminar, he often remains silent at first while he assesses what is going on and the quality of the moderator. He will only speak once he has accessed the event within his own system of values.

Peter is a man of tradition and he acts to preserve it, which at times causes him to be seen as a reactionary. His dress style is classic. His environment reflects the same functionalism and the same organization as Jack's with a touch of culture and classicism (period furniture, antiques, family library, etc.). Peter is very motivated by anything having to do with roots and history. He does extensive research to build his family tree.

He can sometimes "see red" and his anger is as strong as it is brief; what some people call his quick temper. These storms are often inconsequential. They pass. But if his anger falls on Isabelle, it can take her several days to recover from it. Another topic of discord between these two personalities: Peter tends to only see what's wrong, while Isabelle only selects what's right. She often sighs, "He always points out what's wrong and never what's done right." Peter feels that what is done right is normal and that it is important to point out errors in order to make people better. He will more easily commend Isabelle for her humanitarian commitments or non-profit projects than for the quality of her work.

As for changing his opinion, he is naturally suspicious. He enjoys discussing opinions and requires a lot of information in order to change his views.

If Peter does not feel recognized for what he defends, he becomes distressed in a very predictable manner: focusing on other people's mistakes. He becomes more and more rigid. And when it comes to affirming his beliefs, he crusades to the point of becoming intolerant and causing his listeners to turn away.

His existential question is "Am I trustworthy?" and, somewhat paradoxically, he needs time to give his trust.

We find many people with Persister bases in positions of responsibility both in business and in public life, politics, religion, or labor unions. They make up about 10% of the North American population and 75% are male and 25% are female. Some examples of the Persister Base would be; Captain America, Martin Luther King Jr., and Archie Bunker.

Table 1.4: Characteristics of the Persister Type

Character Strengths	Dedicated, observant, conscientious
Characteristics	Expresses opinions, convictions, and judgements
Expresses feelings	Reserved. Believes they are inappropriate in the workplace.
Appearance	Vertical crease between the brows, piercing gaze, classic attire.
Preferred business fields	Entrepreneurial environment. Social affairs. Politics. Religion, Non-profits. Any job with responsibility. The field of security.
Environment	Functional, traditional, period furniture.
Perception	Opinions. Judges, evaluates people and things according to his own opinions.
Team behavior	Likes to take charge. Seeks discussion on opinions. To do so, he more easily seeks a one-on-one relationship over a group, except as a leader.
Psychological needs	To be recognized for his achievements and convictions.

PROMOTER TYPE

Lunchtime: Peter and Jack sit down with their trays in the paneled conference room that Peter is particularly fond of. A relaxing moment. Peter asks Jack:

-   "Do you remember Tom Renaud?"
-   "Yes, the guy who drives a red beamer."
-   "Well, he just filed for bankruptcy. What happened to him is incredible. There's no one like Tom for sniffing out winner markets. A few years back he did a job switch and spent three years in a non-profit working on creating businesses! He got bit by the start-up bug. Naturally, his needs for capital increased considerably and the banks started to get skittish. But as soon as the money came in, he kept forming new companies instead of paying his suppliers. Tom's a funny guy. An adventurer. All he cares about is the challenge. And a quick profit. If he wanted to join us, I'd make him sales manager while keeping a firm hand on the important decisions… But I wouldn't be surprised if he's already got a new project in the works. Truth is, he doesn't

know how to stop." Jack, who has recently become interested in Process Communication Model, smiles, "Your Tom wouldn't happen to be a Promoter, now, would he?"

Jack's diagnosis was perfect. His analysis perfectly fit the trophy rack of the Promoter type.

Give him a challenge, the resources to meet it, the perspective of substantial gains... and he's off and running, preferably at the wheel of his sports car. These three *ingredients* are enough to motivate him. In fact, in thinking of Tom, Peter has often wondered, "But where are his values?"

Tom's value is... action! He cannot sit still for more than two hours without showing signs of impatience or even agitation. His resources: persuasiveness, adaptability, charm, and strong vital energy. His pleasures: luxury goods, expensive clothing, conquest, speed, gambling. Often suntanned (it gives him a better look and he is often athletic), like a playboy he draws you in with his charming smile.

Tom is a go-getter, guided by the Promoter type's existential question: "Am I alive?" he throws himself into action, trusting his instincts to skip the "Thought" part, which places him lightyears away from Jack. If we want to caricaturize Tom and Jack, we could say that Tom would jump onto the train at the risk of realizing later that it was going the wrong way, while Jack would take the time to choose and analyze so much he would miss the train all together. Nonetheless, they form a good team because if the former, for example, would know how to get a business back on its feet, the latter would be indispensable for ensuring its continuity.

What Tom looks for is "incidence", in other words a strong dose of excitement within a short period of time. There is no one like him for seizing opportunities. On the other hand, he has trouble delivering consistent work for long periods of time. Like the people with a Rebel Base, he lives in the moment.

Two things can really irritate him: feelings ("it's for sissies", he might say), and dependency ("I pulled myself up by the bootstrap. People should just do like me."). To put it another way, subtlety is not what he's about and consideration of human problems is not among his hobbies. He is a born loner. Although he makes friends everywhere he goes, he keeps few long-lasting friendships, unless others take the initiative to sustain the relationship. A manipulative side lurks beneath his charm and persuasion. What stimulates him most: anything that resists him. But once the battle is won, he quickly loses interest; he needs new challenges.

If Tom cannot take action and use his combativeness, he can easily vent his frustration by creating tension around him. Making mischief is his usual and predictable distress symptom. As an employee, he likes to have a "firm boss", who makes his field of action clear while letting him act freely within it. If this is not the case, he will easily enter into negative competition and let himself be tempted by intrigue. Using a firm, straightforward tone with him never bothers him, quite the opposite as he likes decisions to be made. Likewise, if he goes through a difficult period, there is no point in showing compassion: for our "Rambo", compassion is the same thing as weakness.

His environment reflects the rule of luxury and gambling, stuffed armchairs, trophies, lots of red and black. When he wants something, it's right now. So he often lives on credit, which creates more tension and negative excitement. Some Promoters can even be qualified as "high rollers", "hotheads", or "a lady's man".

As you may have guessed, their population supplies excellent salespeople and entrepreneurs. They are "rare birds": They represent only 5% of the North American population, 60% are male and 40% are female. Some examples of a Promoter Base are; Captain Kirk from Star Trek, James Bond, and Rambo.

Table 1.5: Characteristics of the Promoter Type

Character Strengths	Adaptable, persuasive, and charming
Characteristics	Ability to be firm and straightforward
Expresses feelings	Rarely. Often sees it as a sign of weakness.
Appearance	Expensive clothing and jewelry that is noticed
Preferred business fields	Sales. Project launches. Sports, Entertainment, Businesses with quick promotion. Challenges
Environment	Luxurious, likes the colors red and black
Perception	Action
Team behavior	Puts in an appearance... likes to act alone. And if he is in a group, it is for action more than for discussion
Psychological needs	Incidence. A strong dose of excitement in within a short time.

IMAGINER TYPE

> "Where did Anne go? We haven't seen her this morning," asks Peter. "You know very well that people don't necessarily see Anne," laughs Joan. "She's probably just in her office." Peter goes to Anne's office. The door is closed. He often enters people's offices without knocking. But with this one, something always seems to hold him back. As if something forced his respect. So he knocks.

He has come to talk to Anne about a document she gave him the day before. A deep, well developed, and quite unexpected text. Peter asks if Anne could speak about it in front of a large audience? Anne seems to recoil at the question. She appears to be daydreaming off somewhere else, "...You know... Yes, of course..." (Silence)... "It would certainly be interesting..." (Silence)... "I'd need some time to prepare..." (Long silence)... "And then, well, developing all of that thought orally... I don't know... It's strange. I don't know if you heard the news this morning, that sudden craze over the Nobel Prize in physics..."

Peter wriggles in his seat. He gets it. There is no point in asking Anne for her opinion. It would be better to ask her directly for her reflection on presenting the document to an audience and leave her sometime to prepare the answer. It is especially important not force her out of her laboratory too soon as she requires that "alone" time to process the question.

Once again, Peter's intuition paid off. Anne has an Imaginer Base. Managing her means respecting her needs in terms of time and solitude, and not forcing her to talk about everything.

Anne is calm, imaginative, and introspective. What strikes people about her first is her "absent" side. She does not seek interaction and can sometimes give the impression of avoiding it.

Her inner life is intense and nothing is reflected on the surface. Her face is smooth, with very few lines, even with age. She chooses her clothing according to comfort or the weather, with no consideration for style, color or esthetics. Her overall look is "natural".

Her workplace, just like her home, is also simple without sophistication. Her surroundings are not very important to her: all she needs is a place to be alone, "to live happily is to live hidden". Her apparent withdrawal does not mean she is uninterested in the people around her. That is just the way she functions. Anne's security is her private world. It is this private world that gives her the unique ability for reflection and introspection.

This is how Anne behaved during a recent seminar: she spoke very little and did not volunteer for role playing or other activities. However, the few times she did speak, her very deep attentiveness and thorough understanding of the method were clear. Always dressed the same unobtrusive way, she used all the breaks to settle into a corner with her nose in a newspaper. At work, she does not particularly enjoy meetings and prefers receiving her staff in her office. Yet, she is still considered as "easy going". The small team she is in charge of has a high degree of independence and plenty of space for initiative and they appreciate the serious way she makes sure information circulates and welcomes all suggestions. On the other hand, chit-chat is not her style. As for asking questions about her private life… Isabelle tried once and still remembers the strange feeling of having spent a few minutes with a "Chinese puzzle".

Anne is comfortable with concrete tasks and manual work that let her pursue her inner travels and that do not require a lot of communication. She needs to receive precise directives and be given freedom in terms of resources. If she is left on her own, she will not take the initiative. For her, action is not vital, she "gets in gear" on stimulation from other people.

She prefers her tranquility over power struggles. Once during a seminar, an Imaginer told us that Imaginers *hate to stand out or be in*

20 • Kahler Communications, Inc.

the spotlight. Also, they are often misunderstood by their superiors who, unlike Peter, do not always understand their essential needs:

> During a seminar, a manager told us of a staff member whom he had nicknamed "Couch Potato". He talked about him angrily, complaining that he never takes any initiative and gets others to do his work for him. Yet, as he described the situation, the manager realized that when he gave the employee specific tasks, they were completed well. The Imaginer Base diagnosis was easy to make and the manager was easily able to draft an action and motivation plan that included precise directives and he stopped expecting the employee to take initiatives.

Her existential question is "Am I wanted?" Now you understand why your Imaginer Base friends do not usually take the initiative to reach out; they don't spontaneously call to see how you are doing and tell you how much it means to them to hear your news.

The Imaginer type makes up about 10% of the North American population, 60% of whom are female and 40% are male. Some examples of the Imaginer Base would be; Albert Einstein, Forest Gump, and Greta Garbo.

Table 1.6: Characteristics of the Imaginer Type

Character Strengths	Imaginative, reflective, calm
Characteristics	Gifted for introspection and imaginative evaluation of people and situations. Enjoys concrete tasks. Working with their hands
Expresses feelings	Rare to non-existent
Appearance	Natural style, practical comfortable clothing
Preferred business fields	Any job requiring solitude and deep reasoning, research, writing, psychology, manual work
Environment	Simple, understated, conducive to inner life
Perception	Inaction/Reflection. Motivated to action by others. Does not take the initiative.
Team behavior	Reserved
Psychological needs	Solitude: a time and space to be themselves

CHAPTER 2

PERSONALITY STRUCTURE

> "Would you mind moving to your Rebel floor? It would give us a break…" whispers Joan. Jack rolls his eyes, "Ever since you did your Process Communication Model seminar you don't miss an opportunity…". "If I recall your "personality condo", your Rebel floor isn't that far from your Base. Come on, try a little harder. Need a tiger in your tank?"
>
> No, Joan is not losing her mind. She is simply integrating – in her own personal way – her knowledge of *Personality Structure*.

TO EACH HIS OWN FLOOR

Each individual has their own "dose" of Harmonizer, Thinker, Rebel, Persister, Promoter, and Imaginer, only in varying amounts of energy and order. Nonetheless, one Type is dominant in each person, the Base Type[3]. And this is true even if during the day a person acts as someone with a Thinker Base by analyzing a problem with his or her reasoning intelligence, or feels like a person with a Harmonizer Base by having a friend over and showing friendship and comfort, or reflects like someone with an Imaginer Base by taking an inward journey, or uses the resources of the Persister floor when they are scandalized by an issue in the paper, or has fun as if they had a Rebel Base.

---

[3] In most people, at some time in their life, certain attributes of another Type will become very important. The process by which this occurs is called "Phasing" or a "Phase Change" and will be discussed later in this chapter.

In the Process Communication Model, each individual's Personality Structure is represented by a six-floor "Condominium", one floor per Personality Type. Each floor has a quantity of available energy. The maximum energy is on the first floor, followed by the others in decreasing order. Let's consider the examples in figure 2.1.

Figure 2.1: Peter and Isabelle: Two Very Different Personality Structures

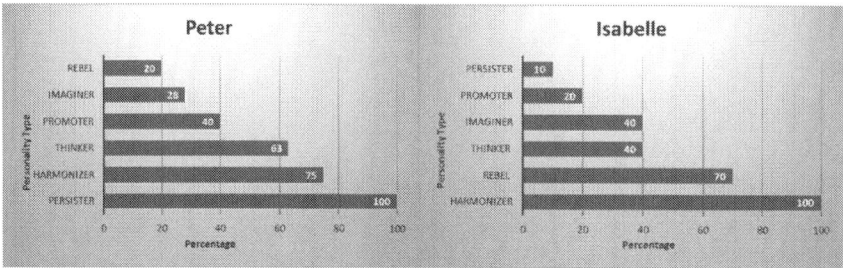

The percentages indicate the relative quantity of available energy at each floor. The lower the percentage, the less a person tends to demonstrate the characteristics specific to that personality type and the more energy that person will need to devote in order to communicate positively with people who present those characteristics.

Here we have two specific personalities among all the possible specific personalities. The number of possible structures is 720 (in other words, 6 x 5 x 4 x 3x 2). If we add all of the various energy levels to this figure, it can be multiplied infinitely… as infinite as the complexity of the human personality.

The first Personality Type (first floor of the Condominium) is called the "Base". According to observations, it seems that this "Base" is innate or acquired within the first months of a child's life and does not change thereafter. So we can say that an individual has a "Harmonizer Base" or a "Thinker Base" but never that the person **is** a Thinker or Harmonizer because an individual is unique and can by no means be reduced to his or her strongest Personality Type. The order of the entire Condominium, in other words, all six floors, is structured by around age seven and appears to be stable.

The Base determines a person's core psychological needs and motivations, the way that person sees the world (the primary Perception), the person's choice of language, the manner in which the person speaks and prefers to be spoken to and a variety of other characteristics.

If we keep the analogy of the Condominium, we can say that each person has an elevator they can use to move up and down. The higher the floor, the less easily a person goes there (the same way an elevator reaches the first floor faster than the sixth). That is why most people more easily occupy the first two or three floors of their Condominium. The secret to communication, regardless of its aim (sales situation, business relations, friendly conversation, etc.), lies in two peoples' ability to "align" with one another, or knowing which button to push to reach the right floor from which to communicate.

> Imagine that someone asks the following question: "Why do we represent this model in the form of a condo?" and that the answer they receive is: "Wow! I love the way you put that question!" The first person would probably open their eyes wide and think, "This guy is weird… and not very serious." What happened? One person was on his Thinker floor, looking for information and the other person on his Rebel floor, reacting. In order to effectively communicate, one of the two should have "climbed" to the other's floor in order to communicate in Rebel mode with the person presenting Rebel or in Thinker mode with the person presenting Thinker. Another scene, same problem: an employee walks into the office of a coworker: "It's so boring around here, let's have some laughs!" The response is: "Finish your work before having some laughs." The employee was speaking from his Rebel floor but the response was given from the Persister floor. If each person sticks to their positions, "watch out for trouble", as a Rebel Base person would say.

If we get to know the different Personality Types, especially those whose traits are not strong within us, and we practice moving up and down the floors of our "Condominium", we will be better able to communicate with others in both our personal and professional lives. If we do not do so, if we stay on our own "comfort" floors[4], it will be difficult for us to maintain relationships with people in whom another

---

[4]   In general, floors with a "strength" of over 60%, which are ones we can visit most easily.

Personality Type is strongest. We will feel we have nothing to say, that communication with this person isn't smooth, or that the other person is from another planet. "Clearly, we're just not wired the same way," said an IT trainee with a Persister Base.

Let's go back to Peter's "Condominium" (figure 2.1). His three "comfort floors" are Persister (his Base), Harmonizer and Thinker. He naturally has the ability to communicate with other Persister Base people and usually can communicate easily with Harmonizer and Thinker Base people. To communicate with Promoter, Imaginer, and Rebel Base people he will have to use more energy.

We can think of the "strength" of a floor in two ways. First, it impacts the ease with which we can access the Type located on that floor. If the strength is under 20% we tend to have a lot of difficulty even moving to that floor. Second, it is a rough measure of the length of time we can remain communicating on that floor before we naturally have to go back to our Base and communicate in the way we are most comfortable. If we do not do that, we can become distressed. If we are attentive to this, we can find our own solutions so as not to break communication, like the case of this manager, "About the time I learned about the Process Communication Model, I had just bought a company that had an IT department. I had never worked with IT people before and I discovered a whole different world filled with artists and poets with whom I had real difficulties communicating. When I saw my Personality Structure, I understood. The Rebel type is at the top floor of my condo, at 10 or 15%... which explained my communication difficulties. I remember coming back from the training session with a new outlook on my "aliens" from R&D. From that day on, everything has gone remarkably well. In terms of meetings, I was careful not to spend a lot of my time with them and I made sure to see them in the morning when I felt in better spirits. I would begin with a few jokes, which put everyone in a good mood and then, after about an hour, when I could feel the stress creeping in, I managed it. When I could no longer manage it, I left. After that, they were able to manage themselves. As for me, by "managing the process", I avoided escalation that could have led us to conflict.

We perceive with our Base, and as Pascal Legrand shows us in this story of one of his experiences as a Process Communication Model trainer, it is usually more natural for us to perceive the positive traits of the Personality Types that are closest to us and, in the same manner, to perceive the negative traits of the Personality Types whose traits we do not strongly share.

Watch your step on the 6th floor

"That morning, I was standing before a dozen operational managers from an industrial corporation. The theme of the training session was "individualize your management and your communication".

The participants' personality inventory results indicated with good statistical validity that they all had Persister/Thinker Bases. The 5th and 6th floors of their Condominiums were Promoter or Imaginer. A typical profile in the industrial world. The time came to present the 6 Personality Types, with video examples. This is what I observed:

- After the presentations of the Harmonizer, Thinker, and Persister types, the trainees' spontaneous comments mainly pertained to the positive characteristics of these three Types.

- However, the first remarks and observations concerning the Promoter and Imaginer types were essentially critical or ironic. For the Promoter Type I heard: "he's such a show-off, an opportunist, thinks only of his image, just talks the talk", etc. For the Imaginer type: "She's off her rocker! She's not connected, sounds like she's out to lunch", etc.

What conclusions can we make from this story?

Some people tell me that the Promoter Type and especially the Imaginer Type are caricaturized or even demeaned. This would explain the clients' negative comments. As for my clients themselves, in construction and industry, they told me that these two Personality Types can never be managers. And the proof is, there aren't any in their firm! I answered that I run into Promoter Base managers in mass retail and Imaginer Base managers in research all the time.

What can we say about these two stories?

I run the Process Communication Model training for an organization whose mission is to help deprived youth with social and professional integration. Both groups of participants are composed of men and women with Harmonizer or Rebel Bases. The 5th or 6th floors of their Condominiums is Persister. I showed them the same video and heard the following comments:

- For the Promoter or Rebel Types: "A lot of our youths have that profile... That's exactly the way they behave."

- For the Persister Type, the first remarks are "He's such a stick in the mud! He's paranoid! He's such a jerk, we couldn't work with him... he's no fun!"

In another service company, the trainees are Promoter and Rebel Base. Their 5th or 6th floors are Harmonizer. The negative comments were mainly aimed at the Harmonizer Type: "She wouldn't last long with us! She's a social worker not an HR manager! Her touchy-feely stuff has no place here!"

I suggest the following conclusion: we first perceive the negative traits of the Personality Type we have the least of (that corresponds to the 5th and 6th floors of our Condominium).

We must be careful of clichés that come from our 6th floor...

I have a Thinker Base. My Promoter is on the 5th floor. For a long time I believed that Promoter type people were all manipulative, opportunistic, without values or long-lasting attachments. Until one day I had a colleague with a Promoter Base who had values, a stable business and private life, and who was able to show empathy and human warmth. His 5th floor was Harmonizer and his 6th was Persister. One of my friends with a Harmonizer Base thinks that people with Persister Bases are "a pain". Her top floor is Persister. So, to conclude, to keep from tripping on the elevator, watch your step on the 6th floor!"

BETWEEN BASE AND PHASE

Earlier we saw that each person has a strongest Personality Type called their "Base" and develops the characteristics of the other five Types during childhood. Most people, at some point in their life, experience a process by which their most important Psychological Needs and motivations, together with how they behave in distress, change to those of a Personality Type other that the Base. When this occurs we say that the person has changed "Phases."

Let's take an example. Albert is a sales manager for Acosix, a small company specializing in precision mechanics, has a Persister Phase. He is a man of opinions with a strong personality who does not hesitate to defend his convictions on how things should be done. He is often perceived as cold and authoritarian, with a highly developed sense of duty and very high standards for both himself and others. Albert is 39 years old, he is married, the father of four children, a practicing Catholic, and campaigns for Amnesty International.

Figure 2.2: Albert's Condominium

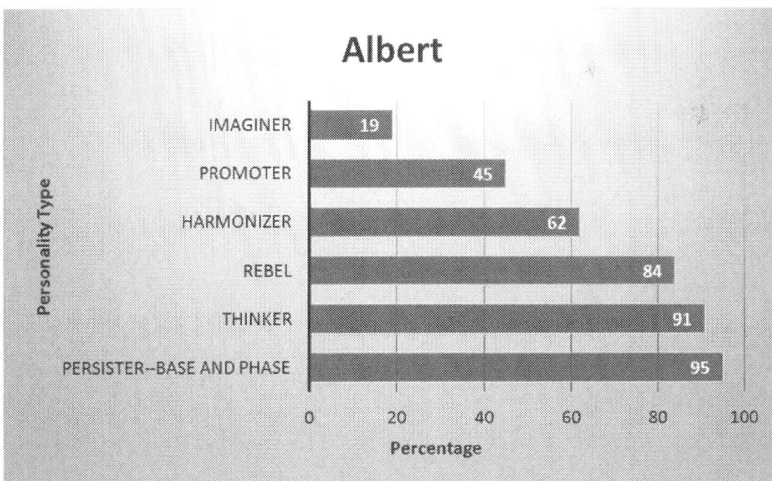

For a while now, his loved ones have noticed changes in behavior. While he still primarily exhibits the traits and language of his Persister Base, He seems more interested in searching for facts and information.

People sometimes point out to him that he is asking questions while before he tended to affirm his opinions right away. He is also developing a good ability to listen (a relatively rare quality among people with a Persister Base and Phase). In other words, more and more, he is showing the traits of a Thinker Type. He seems to have put opinions on the back burner and now tries to support them with concrete data as often as possible. Most importantly, he seems motivated by performance, doing a good job, and keeping to a plan. Now his Personality Structure looks like this:

Figure 2.3: Albert's Condominium After Phase Change

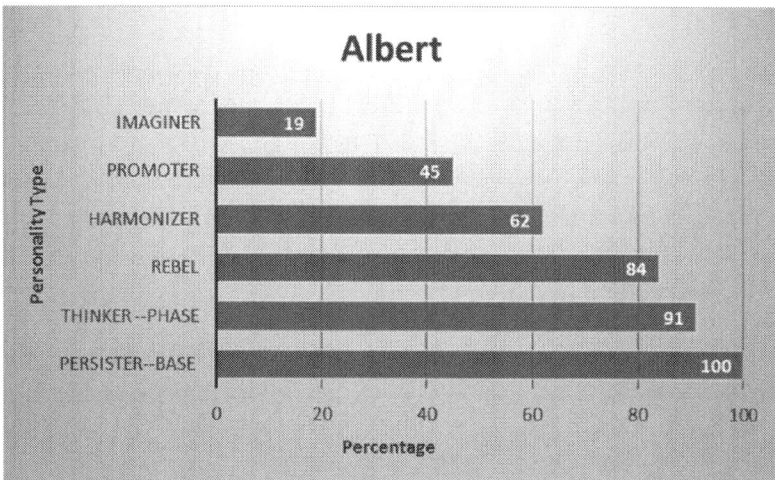

Albert has a Persister Base. He is in Thinker Phase.

Five years go by: we run into Albert with whom we had lost touch. What we first notice is his new look. He has let his hair and mustache grow. His formerly strict cut now looks much more natural. He wears a colored shirt and a very original tie. His attire is unusual and in any case differs considerably from the way we had always known him.

He approaches us with a warm, relaxed "Hi!" and starts by offering coffee and telling a story. While he used to be very serious, he now appears to invite us to joke and play.

Albert has changed Phases again. Now he is in a Rebel Phase, and exhibits more of the traits of that Personality Type.

Figure 2.4: Albert's Condominium After a Second Phase Change

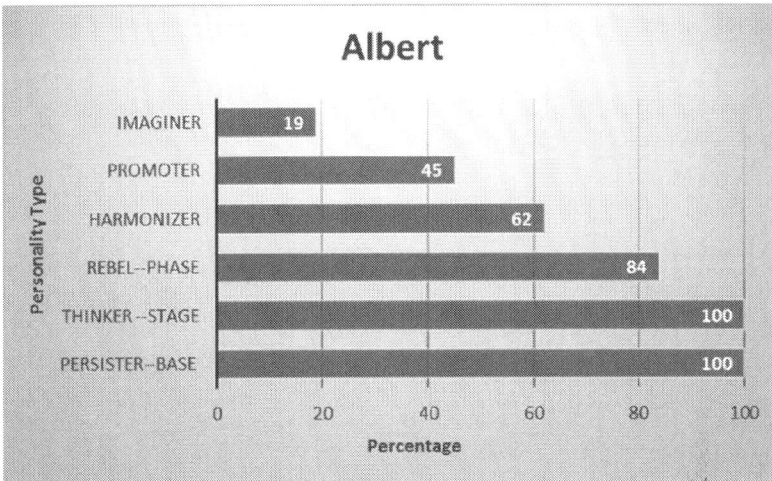

Albert

Personality Type	Percentage
IMAGINER	19
PROMOTER	45
HARMONIZER	62
REBEL--PHASE	84
THINKER--STAGE	100
PERSISTER--BASE	100

What he looks for now in his social interactions? He often starts with a joke, some fun, something pleasant before getting down to serious matters. His adult children describe him as much "cooler" than before. In a way, they even think he resembles Keating, the literature professor in Dead Poets Society! Naturally, behind his playful demeanor, his opinions and convictions can still be detected.

Albert has a Persister Base, has experienced a Thinker Phase and is currently in Rebel Phase. We can predict that, if he changes again (a Phase can last from two years to a lifetime), he will Phase into Harmonizer and exhibit more of the characteristics of the Harmonizer type.

The order of the Phases is always the same: from the bottom to the top of the Condominium, the next Phase being located just above the previous one.

With each Phase change, the immediate Psychological Needs, motivations, sources and manifestations of distress become those of the new Phase, those of the Base reappear rarely, under certain types of stress.

In understanding the model, it is important to distinguish between adapting to the personality of others and a phase change. In the first case, it is a daily process that takes place each time a person "takes their elevator" to respond to the solicitations of their environment, enabling them to adapt to their different interlocutors. In the second case, the person's Psychological Needs, motivations and behavior change durably. This does not keep them from continuing to adapt on a daily basis. Let's take two more examples to illustrate this process.

> Peter (see condominium in figure 2.1) has a Persister Base. He is currently in Harmonizer Phase. His current sources of motivation are being recognized as a person and satisfying his sensory needs. If he changes phases, he will be in Thinker phase. Still loyal to his value system and need for organization, he will try to develop his knowledge and skills more, will attach much more importance to structuring time. In light distress, he will become perfectionist and, in second degree distress, will over-control.

> As for Isabelle (see condominium in figure 2.1), here is how she describes her phase change: While keeping my sense of harmony, I chose more provocative clothing, I still enjoy warm atmospheres but I get bored quickly if we're not having fun, if people "drone" too much. I'm developing my creativity, but I encounter real difficulties in structuring my work and completing long and slightly routine tasks... When I am distressed, I discovered a new ability to "rant" although, when things get really tough, I feel the need to "nourish my base" by spending time with the family or with attentive, reassuring friends (but funny too, please), or enjoying a fine meal at a restaurant, a sauna, etc.

The concept of phase change helps us to understand the meaning of behaviors perceived by others as contradictory. For instance, while a Harmonizer base person's natural tendency is still focused on others, on helping people and listening, if they are in Promoter phase, they will devote most of their time and emotional investment to quick action and business. Or another person with an Imaginer base in Rebel phase will try to "have a blast" with others as much as trying to be alone. It is more helpful to say, "I have an Imaginer base and I am in Rebel phase than, I'm odd, I don't know what I want."

The phase change also helps understand why a friend we haven't seen in years can seem strange. The person's way of being, their vocabulary, and needs have changed and can give the impression that they are someone else. "We're no longer in sync", "We don't have anything in common anymore", "How could I have ever been close to him or her?"

WHAT CAUSES A PHASE CHANGE?

Dr. Kahler discovered the phenomenon of Phase changes and their cause. While a full description of the cause requires a detailed study of psychology and childhood development, it is sufficient for our purposes to say that Phasing occurs when a person is presented with a specific psychological issue, unique to their current Phase, and struggles with dealing with that issue in a healthy way. During the period of struggle, the person exhibits the distress behaviors associated with the Phase Type often and intensely.[5] This happens over time until, finally, the person incorporates the issue – deals with it in a healthy way. At this point, the Phase changes and the prior distress behavior stops. There is neither an advantage nor a disadvantage to a Phase change. In other words, people who have experienced a change are no "better" than those who have remained in their Base. Phasing is not synonymous with instability, just like remaining in one's Base is not a sign of rigidity. They are simply different states.

While the process of Phasing takes place over time, the actual change in Phase and associated characteristics such as Psychological Needs takes place suddenly, when the Phasing process ends. Also, the person's "new" personality is attenuated by their Base, which remains primary in many respects and subsists in the "background" with respect to others. This phenomenon gives attentive observers a chance to draw mixed portraits like the ones we propose now.

---

[5]   This is distinct from the « normal » Phase distress behavior discussed in the book. During the process of Phasing, getting the Psychological Needs of the Phase met positively does not stop the behavior, as it normally does.

Figure 2.5: Jeanne's Condominium

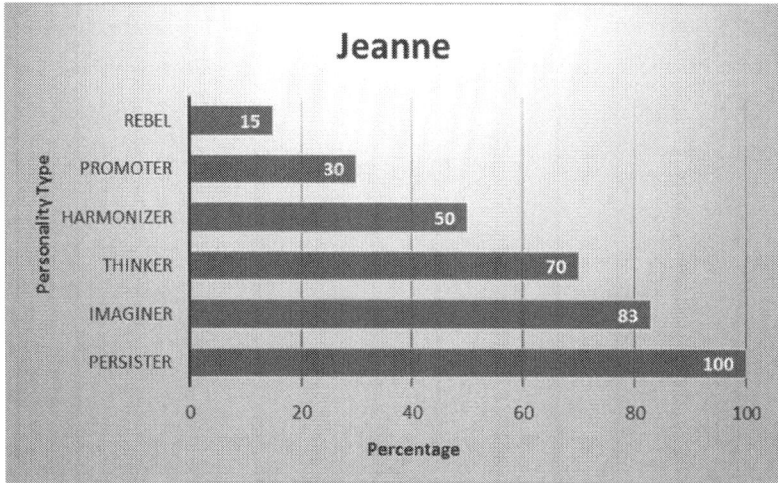

Jeanne, who has a Persister Base and is now in an Imaginer Phase, still has not lost her opinions. When she is behind the wheel, she says, "Let's get moving folks! It's incredible, these people pass when they're not supposed to and this construction work will never end. The way the city schedules this kind of operation is just wrong. Between us, it's just another project designed to make the mayor look good that won't do a thing to make our lives easier."

She is using her opinions in everyday life. However, she is more discreet and reflective. If she is under stress or does not feel on top of her game, she would be the kind to "repair" herself by taking a time out, to try to understand what is happening by herself and enjoy entire days with nothing planned in which she has all the time she needs. That's how Jeanne is: inhabited by a mix of Imaginer and Persister.

She is slow to establish trust but once she gives it, she is a loyal friend. However, we should not expect her to regularly keep in touch. Jeanne does not seek much contact nowadays and prefers quiet walks alone over the long debates she used to be so fond of. Nonetheless, she is very present during encounters with others. Jeanne is a good listener; that is undeniable. Except when her opinions overtake her and she sets out to show the other person what's right in general and what is right for that person in particular. She believes very strongly in mankind and the human ability to change. She can talk for hours about her job – a teaching advisor – with a myriad of details accompanied by ellipses as moments of silence during which to ponder. Yet, she is not a tireless worker. Giving up her free time would lead her straight to depression. When her friend Isabelle doesn't hear from her for two weeks, she thinks, "Jeanne must have a million things to do and tons of people to meet". She is surprised when she learns that her "overworked" friend has been spending long days alone at home.

With company, Jeanne is not the queen of chit-chat. She sometimes gives the impression of pulling her phrases out of a deep hole and offering them up with parsimony as she pulls them up. But all it takes is for the conversation to turn to one of her passions or a topic she has observed and has drawn her conclusions on and she's off... and there is no stopping her. Her tone becomes more affirmed, authority rears its head, as well as the fervor of strongly defended causes. She was a good leader and a great speaker (which she still is on occasion), but now she prefers tranquility.

Figure 2.6: Vincent's Condominium

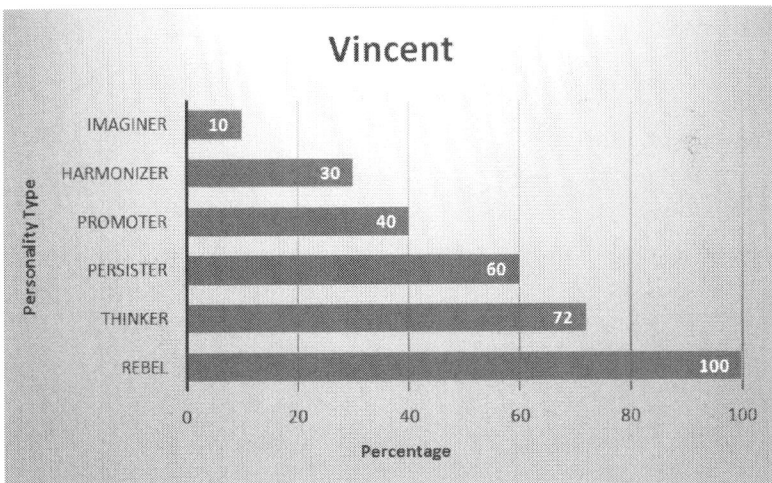

Vincent, age 28, also presents an interesting contrast between his base and his phase:

Vincent frowns. Why did he ever accept this assignment that is clearly beyond his competency? He feels like he is whizzing down the slope of stress at top speed. Of course, he was not working much and needed the money and thought he could handle *everything*: "You are perfect, my boy, aren't you?" "Well, no!" he suddenly rants. He sweats heavily as he studies the survey results he doesn't give a hoot about, "This job will never end and anyway, it's obvious that the client did not do his share… in fact, he ought to get organized. He shouldn't have to delegate stuff like this. Oh, and what the heck, I'll do it tomorrow…" Vincent gets up, gives his cat Vinicius a piece of his mind in a language only the two of them speak. He is getting ready to go downstairs for a cup of coffee at the diner when the telephone rings, probably a girlfriend. Great! Plenty of reasons to have something else to do.

Yet, for a while now, it seems that Vincent is trying to get his life in order. He has filed his papers, decided to make himself a career, is looking for a place of his own instead of sharing an apartment with five or six other buddies. He feels a very strong need for security, wants to deepen his knowledge and be recognized as a specialist. His attitude is an exotic mix: regular hours at the head of an impeccably tidy desk, but he is still a clown whose every gesture sets off peals of laughter. He can no longer stand disorder but systematically drops everything as soon as two buddies gather in the room next door, or when his personal inner clock recommends a coffee break or if the neighbor's kid shows up with a ball under his arm (Vincent was a football star as a teen).

Vincent is the "Master of Fun" at every party. He has a ball making up sketches and suggesting the most outlandish games to his guests. However, he does not at all appreciate it if they arrive late (how could they?) or if they don't play by the rules of those games. Vincent is a well-organized merrymaker. In fact, he has recently found a wonderful way to combine his Rebel Base and his Thinker Phase. He organizes, markets, and runs a training agency in which participants learn team cohesion by spending most of their time playing games!

At this point, you may have several questions, such as:
- How did this theory evolve? To be convinced by these examples, I need to see the demonstration of the model's reliability (Persister)
- How can we obtain the details on a personality structure? How do we define the energy level available for each floor? How can we determine a person's Base and Phase? What is this representation based on? (Thinker)

- A pie chart with colors would be more fun that a condo... why not? (Rebel)
- Hmmm, this tool certainly helps understand others better and to communicate more easily. How can I find out everything about my "Condominium"? (Harmonizer)
- Knowing a person's Phase... there's got to be something you could do with that... (Promoter)
- The interest in this model is that it presents the tremendous complexity of an individual in a very simple way. I'm going to delve deeper into this concept (Imaginer).

The answers to these questions are given in chapter 8 with the presentation of the Profile. As an essential tool in Process Communication Model, the profile results from statistics work conducted by Dr. Taibi Kahler. A carefully calibrated questionnaire, it helps precisely determine an individual's personality structure, the energy level available at each floor of the Condominium, and all of the related characteristics in terms of communication, performance conditions and probable reactions under stress.

THE INTEREST AND IMPORTANCE OF THE FIRST SECONDARY TRAIT[6]

We all know the importance of the base and the phase in the communication and motivation processes. But have you noticed that the first secondary trait after the phase (or after the base for someone who has never changed phases) also has its importance and significance?

Let's take an example:

| 1st Secondary Characteristic PROMOTER |
| Current Phase PERSISTER |
| Base THINKER |

John has a Thinker base and is in a Persister phase. As a training engineer, he has worked for many years as head of production for a small industrial firm. During his Process Communication Model training he mentioned his current professional situation. He told us that he feels satisfied by his job, but that:

- The Monday morning briefings seem too long or even pointless because they do not result in enough concrete actions
- Things are not moving fast enough in his company
- He does not think his manager is firm or straightforward enough
- Decisions could be made more quickly

He also told us that he has a stimulating life outside of work (road rallies, competition fencing).

I asked him whether he planned to switch to a more stimulating job in the future that is more based on action or possibly go into business for himself. He confirmed that in fact he would like to start his own company in order to be freer to operate as he sees fit and live more independently.

CHAPTER 3

ENERGY AND MOTIVATION: PSYCHOLOGICAL NEEDS

"The fundamental task of any manager (…) consists in driving positive emotions among those he or she manages." Daniel Goleman

One or two distinct Psychological Needs correspond to each Personality Type. This aspect is among the key points of the Process Communication Model: Taibi Kahler's work established that satisfying the Psychological Needs of the Phase is an essential source of motivation. An individual's energy level under "normal" physical and psychological conditions largely depends on this satisfaction.

Isabelle – "He doesn't say hello to me any more… he's upset… I'm sure something's wrong. I wonder what I did? Things are getting off to a bad start and I don't have a good feeling about this. It was too good to last. I should have guessed…"

Joan – "I don't feel like it, it's hard, it's all so dull; these people bore me. I've had it. This thing is giving me a headache. It interested me at first but now I feel like I'll never get to the end of it. I feel like sending it all packing. I'm not in the mood to work… it's only been fifteen minutes? All that time left to go on this nightmare!"

Tom – "Oh, hi Peter, you're a pal…. Hey, I just heard something; I'll tell you since I think a lot of you. At the last executive committee meeting the boss really smeared you.…"

Peter – "They don't trust me; they don't listen to me anymore. No one asks my advice anymore… My word, they're benching me already. At my age.…"

Anne – "Silence. Absence. Emptiness. Nothing.…"

Jack – "My friends tell me I should go away for a weekend…. That's impossible. I haven't finished working on this file. In fact I'm sure there are one or two mistakes in it. I absolutely must find them. I'll take everything home with me tonight. Anyway, I couldn't relax until I've finished…. I'm the only one who can do this…."

A few moments later:

- Hello, Isabelle, how are you? It's always a pleasure to see you. You're irreplaceable… (Isabelle laughs)
  o No…. I'm just fine thank you. And you? Would you like some coffee?

- Hey, Joan, what's up?! I brought some great info back from Bismack and they gave me tons of exciting material…. By the way, did you get to the movies last night?"
  o Yeah, it was great. I've gotta tell you about it…. I'll be right over. Let's have a look at those materials. Wow! I feel really jazzed up all of a sudden.

- Hey, Tom, this is no time for sleeping. The folks at Bismack just called. Go over and negotiate a new deal!
  o I'm on my way! Finally, things are moving! I was starting to get moldy….

- Dear Peter, you know how much I value your commitment to the company. What do you believe are the best solutions? (Peter sits up straight, his face lights up).
  o Really? Thanks. Actually, I thought that…in fact I have several ideas.

- Anne, you know, you don't really have stay here with us. The main thing is that I can get the information to you tomorrow. (With a smile of relief, Anne finally speaks).
  o Thank you, that's really nice of you. You can count on me tomorrow for the follow-up.

- Jack, you've done an excellent job and we really appreciate it (Jack's expression relaxes).

o   Thank you. I was thinking of finishing the Duval file over the weekend, but I realize that we'll have more information on Monday. It would be best to wait.

What happened here? The right words, the right attitude "recharged the batteries" of each of the protagonists. What batteries? The Psychological Needs batteries. What touched Isabelle was a gesture, some special attention. What stimulated Joan was an avalanche of "fun" proposals, while the arrival of an exciting project is what turned Tom's lights on.

Let's imagine that nothing had happened. It is probable that each protagonist would have continued their distress behavior, at the risk of harming their work or relationships. This is what we call the *search for negative satisfaction* of Psychological Needs. Since childhood, we have all learned that *it is better to receive negative attention than no attention at all.*

Some behavior in business or private life can seem illogical or incoherent. For example, one person interrupts curtly and tries to impose his point of view. Another suddenly seems to have lost her bearings, is no longer able to think on her own and gives exasperating answers. Or another might unleash her creativity, but in bad faith. Yet another might take perverse pleasure in pitting people against one another. Lastly, a coworker is unable to pull himself away from his files and feels the need to verify everything he is told. Popular wisdom teaches the art of putting meaning behind, or rather, labeling these behaviors, to reassure ourselves: the first person is a "more or less enlightened" despot, the second "plays dumb", the third seems to "beg for a kick in the pants", the fourth plays "duke it out", and the last over-controls and allows himself to be consumed by his work[7].

All of these behaviors indicate that the individual is distressed and seeking satisfaction of his or her needs in a negative way. When distressed, we no longer think clearly and consequently we are often unaware of our negative behavior.

Readers who want experimental proof of the real meaning of our negative behavior may read the experiences below after making sure they are taking a sincere, benevolent approach.

---

[7]   Eric Berne, *The Games People Play.*

If they show understanding and respect towards a person who abruptly interrupts and tries to impose their views, the "despot" will immediately relax and recover his ability to listen and be open to real communication.

If they show warmth, understanding, and reassurance to the exasperating person who "plays dumb", in a fraction of a second, their interlocutor's IQ will seem to jump 50 fifty points.

If, in dealing with the creative in bad faith, they are able to relax, smile, and even joke a bit, a miracle with occur; they will be able to laugh together and as if by magic, the person will recover her sense of responsibility.

As for the troublemaker, by proposing that he invest his energy in a new challenge, the atmosphere will improve instantly.

Finally, if they are able to recognize the abilities and work delivered by the last character and reassure that person and appeal to his sense of responsibility, they will be able to encourage him to relax and enjoy a pleasant moment together.

Are you ready to try this? Bravo. Understanding these human mechanisms will be a source of deep satisfaction for you. Are you still skeptical? We suggest taking a deeper look at the description of each Personality Type's Psychological Needs and, for each one of them, discover the related behavior of their non-satisfaction.

NEEDS OF THE HARMONIZER

Two types of needs are prerequisites for the Harmonizer to enjoy a good level of energy.

Feeling recognized as a person, in other words, appreciated for who they are and not what they do. All positive signs of recognition invite them to feel good and particularly recharge them. For instance, *"I feel good with you"*, *"We're lucky to have you with us"*, *"You contribute to the good atmosphere on the team"*. In these examples we do not target what the person does, but who she is.

A greeting and personal availability are the daily bread of Harmonizer type people. But, you might object, isn't it everyone's? Of course, but the lack of these does not invite immediate discomfort or a behavioral change in everyone.

During a seminar with a team from a rapidly growing garden center, we noted that the caterer had a Harmonizer

Base. He was very attentive to his customers and the atmosphere, decoration, and kindness he showed to diners were Harmonizer-like.

During a break, he was talking to the garden center manager and told him that, as a customer, he reminisced the days when the center was small and how it made him feel better. Now that it so much larger he feels lost. For example, when the center was small, he could select his plants, put them in his basket and then maybe see some others that were more suitable, change his mind, hesitate, etc. Now, in the larger center, when he asks a hostess for information, she uses a microphone to call a technician and, he concluded, "She abandons me". After five minutes of feeling alone and frustrated, he left, promising himself that next time he would go to a smaller competitor with a more human touch.

Sensorial needs. For the Harmonizer type, the five senses are the main source of self-renewal. Good examples of these are: colors, flavors, fragrances, music, sensations from a massage, a sauna or the sun, and a soft woolen sweater. In other words, the whole range of senses is able to restore the person's good mood. On the flip side the lack of pampering of the senses to the Harmonizer will result in negative performance. If you give a Harmonizer a dark office furnished with metal filing cabinets and only a dusty window decorated with a row of computers and a fireman's calendar, you risk seeing that person wither like a forgotten plant!

Negative Satisfaction

When deprived of unconditional recognition, people with a Harmonizer Base become distressed and try to satisfy these needs negatively. They tend to "overdo it" by pleasing others, with the unconscious aim of being rejected, and they make mistakes. The *"Are you stupid, or what?"* that can sometimes be heard all the way down the corridors of some companies often comes from an exasperated manager towards a desperate Harmonizer worker.

In the event of sensorial needs that are not positively satisfied, Harmonizer type people tend to "take revenge" by over eating and failing to take care of their appearance.

NEEDS OF THE THINKER

Positive satisfaction of two needs will contribute to the efficiency of the Thinker.

Recognition of their work: a Thinker knows that the task they have just completed is well done. They have enough knowledge of their intellectual and organizational abilities to be able to assess this. But if that person does not receive a few words of encouragement such as, "*This report meets our expectations. It even goes beyond what we could have hoped for. Congratulations!*" or "*I particularly appreciate the quality of your work*", then, without even realizing it, that person will become frustrated. Receiving regular feedback is a real source of performance for these people.

A young journalist with a Rebel Base in Thinker Phase tells us, "On my first job I was asked to conduct a survey that was a real headache on the topic of Europe. I worked like a madman for an entire month and handed in my report. After a week, I still hadn't received any feedback and I began to feel disappointed, disenchanted, and worried. It was impossible for me to get involved with a new project; my "batteries" were depleted. Until one day when I ran into my boss on the stairway. All it took was a second. "Your article was fantastic," he told me, "exactly what we needed!" All of my energy came back in an instant. All of my problems went away and I got back to work with a vengeance."

Frequently, Thinkers have learned to be wary of signs of recognition because they have observed very early on that when their work is recognized, they are asked to do more. For example: "*I know I can count on you, so could you just change this...*" or "*Since you have such a good ability to summarize and be concise, I'd like you to...*". They already heard the same kinds of remarks in childhood: "*Look after your brother since you're the mature one.*"

Structuring time: "Until when? For how long? What do we do after that? What time is breakfast? And next Thursday's meeting?" These are all important questions for Thinker type people. And when asked, they are able to answer easily since they are usually very well organized. They immediately look for these markers when they join a new structure; even their vacations are usually carefully planned out.

Negative Satisfaction

If the need for recognition of their work is not satisfied, the Thinker enters into a progressive process of distress. To compensate for this deficiency and alleviate the doubt that arises, they feel the need to be better than perfect, get bogged down in details, over-qualify, and no longer delegate. They tend to think they can do a better job than others who, in response, take their distance or enter into negative competition. They try to assume all responsibility, which slows activity and they do not usually realize they are distressed. This overinvestment in the professional sphere can cause problems in their private lives that can go as far as the "Post-It syndrome":

> Jack, who has a Thinker Base, comes home from work very late as usual. He finds a Post It on the refrigerator door: "The kids needed a dad to be here and play with them. I wanted a husband who loved me… We have left".
>
> Jack doesn't understand: "It's true that I work a lot, but it's so my family doesn't have to go without"[8].

In their activities, the Thinker's tendency for excessive detail makes them less and less able to communicate clearly: while their concern is to be understood, they confuse others by drowning them with details.

Let's take the example of a trainer with a Thinker Base under light distress who is teaching the Psychological Needs:

> "When we talk about Psychological Needs and in this case, it is important to recall that it is component number 4 of the program we began this morning and for memory, I remind you that the first three chapters were, first of all, the management styles, in which we experimented with the

---

[8]   Analysis of the wife's reaction: with a Harmonizer Base, she has always "sacrificed herself" for the well-being of others. She phased into Rebel and decided, "I exist, too, and I want to fulfill myself". And she began to "live for herself".

appropriate and inappropriate styles for each personality type, and remembering that Alan gave us that extremely interesting experience…"

If the Thinker cannot structure her time as she wishes, she also begins to become rigid on the issue: "I don't understand how that guy can be systematically late. I think we should sanction him. How is it possible to not be able to stick to an agenda and be so poorly organized?"

Understanding the origin of these "tensions" can provide relief and give the person back all of their freedom of action. This was the case for a seminar participant called Nicholas:

> A training center for social workers had asked us to intervene during a three-day seminar. It was geared towards educators who wanted to go over their practices. Some of them had prepared the program they wanted to go over. Their management had added a Process Communication Model day without asking for their opinion.
>
> When we arrived, one of the trainees reacted very aggressively: "Come on, who do they think we are? We didn't ask for this, etc." We "managed the relationship" with him and he calmed down but was still frustrated and did not speak very much. During the presentation of Psychological Needs and their negative satisfaction, he spoke out, "I get it! I've been angry since this morning because this day was unplanned. They didn't take what we had prepared into account. I'll work it out with the center manager. Meanwhile, now that I understand what happened with me, I can pay attention to what's being said here."

NEEDS OF THE PERSISTER

The motivation for this Personality Type comes from their convictions. They devote themselves to what they believe to be the right choice for themselves and for society in general. Consequently, being recognized for their convictions is their major Psychological Need, accompanied by recognition for their work and contributions, just like for the Thinker. It is important for this type to know they inspire trust and that their ideas are sought and appreciated. They "must" be asked their opinion.

Do not hesitate to solicit them as follows: "*What do you believe...?*", "*What is your opinion on...?*", "*Your suggestions interest me*", "*What would you do in my place?*"

The very best would be to say: "*You're right...*" But what if you do not share their convictions? There is a "magic formula" that will keep the conversation from souring: "*That's your opinion and I respect it[9], and I do not agree.*" Even the most dogged person would be sensitive to this sign of attention. However, this kind of "technique" can be seen as manipulative: satisfying the other's Psychological Needs will only be effective if you totally agree with what you say or do. Sincerity and authenticity are the indispensable ingredients to communication.

The need for recognition of their convictions is behind one of the most classic models of conflict on a team. Speaker number one begins: "I'm convinced that we should go about it like this." A coworker with different beliefs would probably answer: "Not at all, I'm certain that it's just the opposite." Within a second, both speakers will become distressed and will no longer listen to each other. While it appears that only beliefs are at stake, in fact, for each of them it is a matter of "winning" in order to receive the recognition they need. And we find ourselves in the troubled waters of negative satisfaction of the need to be recognized for their beliefs.

Negative Satisfaction

If a person in Persister Phase is not getting his need for convictions or recognition of work met, he will tend to seek negative attention in his own way. More than ever affirmed in their position(s), they will rigidly defend their principles and pay more attention to people's errors instead of their successes. They will crusade to defend their case.

> Gentlemen, I think I have clearly demonstrated how essential it is now to meet your staff's Psychological Needs. In fact,

---

[9]   The natural tendency is to say "but", which cancels what has just been said. Using the word "and" is important because it adds useful information.

I expect you to apply this immediately and I demand a comprehensive, detailed report on all of the actions you have taken concerning this managerial strategy which I want to see applied in my company from now on…

In the best of cases, the manager who crusades like this will cause his or her staff to tune out. They will think: *"He'll tell us when he's finished. It goes in one ear and out the other."* In any case, the manager's message does not get through, even if he is absolutely right. He also risks "snagging" a coworker with the same Psychological Need who also begins to crusade: *"What right do you have and what do you base your affirmations on?"* or on an employee with a Rebel base under negative stress: *"Keep talking buddy…"*

NEEDS OF THE REBEL

The main Psychological Need of the Rebel is playful contact. During a seminar in the midst of a group of mainly Persisters and Thinkers, including the trainer, who is not very sensitive to repeated joking, this type has a high risk of leaving before the break. As for the obligation to remain alone in an office for a long time, there is a high chance of its leading to a hefty phone bill…

Rebels need to play, laugh, and work outside the box before getting into it. A serious topic that is addressed straight forwardly will seem like watching paint dry: A Rebel will either quit or seek every means to not feel bored, even to the extreme.

A frequent family situation: The dad with a Thinker Base tells his Rebel daughter when she gets home from school: "Go up to your room and do your homework. You can play later". While this model works with his other children, with this one, it is a complete disaster. It's true that her need is the opposite of her father's. Whether he is a Thinker or a Persister, he feels it is natural (he would say normal) to begin by doing what needs to be done and only then have fun, if there is time. For the young Rebel it is just the opposite: she needs to be "energized" by playing before getting down to serious things. Little by little, homework becomes a formidable chore, not just for her but (especially) for her parents, unless she can do serious things while having fun!

Negative Satisfaction

If the need for contact is not satisfied positively, the person becomes distressed. She complains. A lot. And she blames with every opportunity. Provoking, shocking, she does exactly what should not be done, etc… so as to get her dose of contact through criticism or opposition. A human resources manager related the following misadventure:

> I was presenting a training program to the executive committee in the presence of the CEO. Very soon, one of my colleagues began to systematically contradict me. I thought, "He's trying to show off. I'll just pretend he isn't there." A painful mistake because the colleague "kept insisting and contradicting me more and more, to the extent that I lost my bearings. It was an extremely uncomfortable situation that I have a very bad memory of. Afterwards, I asked him: "What got into you? Why did you act that way?" "Nothing much, I just wanted to see how you would react," he answered.

This behavior is typical of a Rebel seeking attention. He did not receive it and began to "pile it on" to force the other person to notice him. Which illustrates a comment heard in a teen shelter: *"Here, you have to get into trouble for anybody to pay attention to you!"*

NEEDS OF THE PROMOTER

Excitement is a drug for this Personality Type. It is their essential need and systematic source of renewal: a new project that promises quick results, something to build, an athletic competition, a night at the casino, etc… In other words, anything that moves and delivers immediate results. Challenges and concrete action: "There are some big bucks to be made here…"

This need is probably more difficult to satisfy positively over a long period of time because by nature, only something new is exciting. The

Promoter naturally seeks limits and very often enjoys seeing how far he can go, and beyond. Even if their situation does not take them on spectacular adventures, Promoters will try to "make temperatures rise". That is the case of this business school student who explained:

> "For me, what's exciting is the night before an exam, when everyone else is asleep, to sit down at my desk and spend the night reviewing the curriculum for the entire year. I love to know that others are sleeping while I'm at work…and that I'm in the home stretch."

Some Promoters will need to reach the final limit to feel motivated and produce. It is even possible for some to "make the temperature rise" by applying the Process Communication Model. During a follow-up session, a manager with a Persister Base in Promoter Phase who had explored the relational difficulties he had with his boss, told us the following:

During the seminar, I became aware of the "pleasure" I got from being in conflict with my superior. It's true that it was negative excitement for me. Now, what turns me on most is managing the process with him and recognizing him for his opinions. It's amazing to see how much his behavior has changed! In fact, I think that, deep down, what I like most is when he still shows surprise at the change in our relationship.

Negative Satisfaction

For want of action, the person can give in to the joys of making mischief. In this case, there is no one better for manipulating others and creating discord on the team: "Things are finally getting shaken up"[10]. The person will also take excessive risks: abuse of stimulants, speeding, playing the "high roller" in gambling, being headstrong, carrying on several love relationships at the same time, borrowing money and not paying it back on time: "I'm buying. I'll figure out a way to pay it back later."

---

[10] The "grapevine" phenomenon is a problem that most companies suffer from as an expression of the frustration and lack of positive stimulation in the concerned personnel. It becomes "exciting" to start rumors, watch other peoples' reactions and manipulate them.

A distressed person with a Promoter Phase might borrow money from a friend. He/She assures them weekly that he /she will reimburse them soon. When the Promoter Phase receives the money he/she could gamble with it at a casino, to make more money. Then, lose the money and ask for more money from his/her friend and a make another fake promise to reimburse the money soon.

NEEDS OF THE IMAGINER

Solitude. A silent person standing before a painting that beckons quiet and meditation: that is how we can imagine the Psychological Needs of our Imaginer. Perhaps you feel a form of friendliness or respect for that person? Isn't there that kind of special place in each of us, known only to us, where we like to go sometimes to spend a few precious moments? The difference is that, for this Personality Type, there is no "sometimes". These precious moments are frequent and indispensable to their daily psychological balance.

> The archetype of the Imaginer type could be this taciturn artisan who recently came to Peter's house to restore a family heirloom: he got down to work with a sort of silent tranquility that remained with him throughout the day. During coffee, Peter understood that conversation would be brief and that trying to prolong it would make the man uncomfortable. By evening, the work was finished and the man left… with his mystery.

There are different kinds of solitude. The kind for the Harmonizer type is inhabited by feelings for others or a significant other. The kind for the Thinker and Persister types helps them review their current projects or particular issues. The kind for the Rebel type is quite relative: there is usually music and the telephone rings often and the kind for the Promoter type is experienced in action and is fueled by strong sensations.

While the Imaginer type will more easily escape through solitude, opening to spaces of meditation and letting their imaginations roam free, the Imaginer Base is often difficult to identify. The reason is that they try to go unnoticed, as illustrated by these two stories:

Patrick is an accountant and at work he expresses many of the traits of the Thinker type: precise, organized, communicating preferably through facts and practical information. During a Process Communication Model seminar he positions himself as an Imaginer Base and his PPI confirms this evaluation (Imaginer Base and Phase, then Thinker and Persister). His comments:

> *"It's true that I have an Imaginer Base. I need moments of solitude. I organize myself so as not to have more than four or five appointments a day and this is very important to me. The most difficult period is when we remit the year-end statements and I see six or seven clients every day. In this case, I imperatively need at least fifteen minutes between clients."*

As for Philip, he enters into Harmonizer relational mode as soon as he is in contact with other people. He also has an Imaginer Base and Phase. During the seminar, he explained: *"Being on good terms with everyone and making sure things go smoothly without rocking the boat is the best way I have found to live in peace. I also need long moments of solitude. In fact, I live with my girlfriend on a houseboat where I've set up a little corner for myself."*

Negative Satisfaction

If the Imaginer employee is deprived of time and tranquility, he or she tends to begin several projects they do not complete, as if they were desperately trying to harness the passing minutes and get discouraged in the middle. If they are subject to too many contacts, they withdraw, protect themselves, offer even less information about themselves and end up being depressed. When he studied the Psychological Need for solitude, one manager observed:

> Okay, I have just understood the behavior of one of my staff. He worked on a production line and had extremely frequent interactions with his coworkers. Little by little, they lost sight of him. He would disappear without a word and I became aware of the problem because his coworkers started to complain of having take on his workload. Then

he began calling in sick. In desperation, we transferred him to another very independent position where at least his absenteeism would no longer be a problem for his team. He found himself alone at a desk. His behavior entirely changed overnight. He became efficient and reliable. No more sick leave, and since we didn't understand the reasons for the change, we concluded that he must be in love.

Clearly, this employee suffered from an overdose of stimulation in his former environment and had become distressed. In the second phase, he found conditions that satisfied his needs and recovered an excellent level of energy and motivation.

THE HIERARCHY OF PSYCHOLOGICAL NEEDS

Finding motivation by satisfying the Psychological Needs of our Phase does not mean that we do not have other needs. It is just that those needs are not expressed in the same proportions:

John has a Harmonizer Base and is in Promoter Phase. His tendency is to over-stimulate himself, to "overdo it". He recently felt the need for a time out and spent a few days on his own in the country. This is a typical need of the Imaginer floor, which is the last floor of his condominium. As soon as he arrived, he thought, *"It's nice to be alone without a telephone, to have time to read and think, etc. And the countryside is magnificent..."* But very soon, he also thought, *"Okay, that's all well and good, but what do I do now?"* This last sentence tells us that, although John was in contact with his need for solitude, this need was quickly satisfied since he does not have a lot of energy on his Imaginer floor. At that point, John felt the needs of his Phase. But, except during the summer rush, the countryside isn't exactly an exciting place for his Promoter side. He had two solutions: finding positive ways to meet his need for excitement or leave. But imagine if John did neither: he would start to feel tired. Then, little by little, lethargy would start to overtake him. His energy would drop, he would no longer be in the mood for anything and could even feel depressed.

What occurred here? John's essential source of energy and motivation currently comes from the positive satisfaction of the need for excitement – a characteristic of his Promoter Phase. As he is deprived of this, he first enters light stress, showing the negative behavior of his Phase. Then, if his needs are still not satisfied, he sinks into third degree distress.

In fact, each of us can feel all of the different Psychological Needs but at variable intensities. The more the need corresponds to a high floor of our condominium, the more quickly it will be satisfied. The current need then becomes the need of our Phase. In the example of John, that is why he feels little attraction to quiet, solitary activities and tries to avoid those kinds of situations. He would not be a good candidate for a solo trip around the world. He needs to meet people with whom he feels good (Harmonizer Base) and to find challenges, excitement and change (Promoter Phase).

ACCEPTING OUR PSYCHOLOGICAL NEEDS

Satisfying Psychological Needs often means giving or receiving positive signs of recognition[11], which many people have difficulty doing and for a reason: their upbringing and the culture of their environments do not encourage this. They must learn to listen to themselves and give themselves "permission". Let's take the example of Jack, with a Thinker Base:

> During the wrap-up of a particularly successful seminar which he had taken the responsibility to organize, the human resources manager warmly congratulated Jack. His face lit up in a broad smile and he said thank you. Then the administrative and financial manager added his praise. Jack continued to thank him. His smile faded somewhat. Finally, it was the marketing manager's turn. At

---

[11] Only the sensorial needs for solitude and excitement, to a lesser extent, do not require the exchange of signs of recognition. [What about the Time Structure and Sensory needs? They don't require recognition either]

this point, Jack seemed a bit tense and showed discomfort and embarrassment. Clearly, he had trouble accepting the overdose of recognition. Instead of taking advantage of it to maintain a high energy level, he hung out the "no vacancy" sign.

Many businesses have invested considerable dollars in management training and communication and the results can sometimes be disappointing. Yet, many of these courses are well designed and provide managers with a series of techniques to make them more efficient. Most stress the efficiency of positive signs of recognition. However, it is one thing to explain to a participant that those around him or her need such signs and quite another to ensure that the person is psychologically ready to give and receive them.

The training group is a place where it is possible to practice exchanging these signs. It is easy to observe how strong the fear of overdose and manipulation is. Furthermore, if a manager changes his or her behavior, they risk being at odds with the usual practices within the company. Many managers call signs of recognition "sucking up". We can also hear remarks like, "My boss stroked my ego" or "Can you still fit that big head through the door?" All of these reactions show the distance yet to be run to exchange essential words that lead to needs satisfaction and motivation.

The absence of signs of recognition results in a shortage in which people adapt in order to survive and in which they usually function with a low level of energy, on the order of: "The less I do, the better off I am".

The work involved in the Process Communication Model does not only consist in acquiring communication and motivation techniques. In most cases, it must be part of a personal endeavor in which the person is attentive to their own developmental barriers and are able to give themselves permission to meet other people's psychological needs and also receive responses to their own. In a corporate setting, the manager's action plan will take the individual's structure and level of development into consideration[12].

---

[12]   See chapter 9, Process Communication: tailored management

Table 3.1: Psychological Needs

Types	Needs	Negative Satisfaction
Harmonizer	Recognition of person Sensorial needs	Self-deprecation, mistakes Neglect or excessiveness
Thinker	Recognition of work Time Structure	Strive to be perfect Over-control, no longer delegate Over-control others
Persister	Conviction Recognition of work	Same + tendency to only see others' mistakes. Impose their beliefs, Preach
Imaginer	Solitude	Withdrawal
Rebel	Contact	Blame or cause themselves to be blamed
Promoter	Excitement	Excessive risk taking

In the case of miscommunication (conflict, discomfort, or passivity), we can easily see how to offer the psychological needs to invite back to communication. During our seminar, to practice this concept, we suggest a role play in which they play out anger, blame, sadness, etc. They soon realize that, after two or three exchanges offering them right psychological needs, they are unable to play their role and emerge from miscommunication. Here is an example with a crusade and need of conviction:

- I think it's scandalous! No one ever listens to me.
- Do you want to tell me the reasons why you are angry?
- The reasons! The reasons! The reasons are simple: yesterday I pointed out how far behind we are and that it was crucial to manage this client situation immediately.
- I understand your frustration over not being listened to. It's true that you've been following the matter very closely. Now, would you accept to reconsider this situation with us so that we can manage it better?
- Yes, of course.

CHAPTER 4

WAVELENGTHS

"In the era of globalization, the relationship with others is more fundamental than ever."

-Dominique Moïsi

Peter bursts into Isabelle's office. "Hi, make me a summary of this file. Also correct this letter for me because I would like it to go out today."

Isabelle is worried this morning. She has just had two unhappy customers on the phone. "You really treat me like a machine," she stammers. "What have I done now?"

Peter looks at her with surprise. He is especially confused since he has just spoken to Anne in the same tone and she did not show any dismay.

What happened here? Peter and Isabelle are clearly not on the same wavelength. Each of them is competent and is right for his or her job. There is no reason why they should not be able to work together, it's that they do not understand each other. If we suppose that each of them sticks to their positions, they could very well enter into conflict. This situation occurs every day with millions of people around the world and causes a considerable waste of energy. It usually results in remarks like, "He doesn't understand anything", "Who does she think she is?", "I'm not getting through..." etc. Regardless of the importance of the content to be transmitted, if the form in which it is said is not receivable by the interlocutor, it has little chance of coming across effectively.

Each personality type has its own unique form of expression and preferred communication style. Each type's style is expressed through the preferential use of a "communication channel". This channel is the unique wavelength that each personality type naturally tends to use to communicate. Likewise, each type also prefers to be addressed on that same frequency. We also define the communication channel as the encounter of two personality parts. These personality parts were discovered by Dr. Taibi Kahler and are called Protector, Director, Computer, Comforter and Emoter. In order for there to be communication, it is necessary that each speaker uses a complementary personality part to establish a communication channel. A set of characteristics, known as "behavioral cues" makes up each "part"; which includes choice of words, tone of voice, gestures, posture, and facial expressions.

A communication channel exists when someone "offers" a personality part to which the other person is receptive and the other person responds with an associated personality part. This is a basis for effective communication.

PERSONALITY PARTS

Protector

This is a parental part of the personality that gives orders aimed at the other's sensory part, "breathe, calm down, listen to me, look at me." These directions come from the Protector and do not contain attacks, threats, or anger. They address the five senses. The tone of voice and posture are firm and calm, hands and arms held forward. The facial expression conveys trust and support. The Protector is particularly appropriate for situations involving loss of self-control or excessive anxiety. It is not linked to any particular personality type.

Using it for one's self is a good way to alleviate situations of embarrassment, frustration, or confusion and start thinking clearly again. Using the Protector part increases the chances of solving problems and taking care of one's self. Instructors use the Protector part during relaxation sessions: "Breathe deeply, relax…"

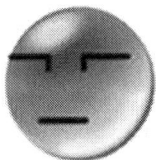

Director

When Tom, who has a Promoter base uses his Director part, he gives orders aimed at the thinking part of his interlocutor. His directives "Tell me", "Explain to me", and "Do" invite the other person to think and/or act. His attitude bears no anger, attack, or threat. His tone is firm and calm, gestures are rare, his posture is straight and he has no particular facial expression. This part naturally is used at the Promoter floor.

Computer

The computer is the individual's thinking part. Its function is to ask, process or deliver information. It enables people to communicate very efficiently. Questions and answers are worded very clearly and usefully, with no show of emotion. The tone of voice is neutral, posture straight and calm with no particular gestures or facial expression. Example: "What time is it?", "Have I answered your question?"

Jack uses this personality part to receive information and process it verbally and logically ("That's what communication is for, isn't it?"). Peter also uses it, only the information will be chosen to enrich his frame of reference. To find out the other person's opinions, for instance. Anne finds all of the tools to proceed with an in-depth analysis of situations using the Computer part. She also uses it to perform tasks that others would find boring.

Thinker, Persister, and Imaginer types are the primary users of the Computer part.

Comforter

This personality part addresses emotions and feelings in a warm, nurturing way. Isabelle prefers using it; it is how she shows her concern or appreciation for others. A few typical phrases from the Comforter part: "It's wonderful having you with us", "I enjoy working with you", "I am touched by your concern". It enables the person addressed to feel recognized as a person.

The Comforter gestures are invitations: extended arms, open palms, or one hand on the other person's arm or shoulder. The tone of voice is soft and warm, posture is relaxed and comfortable, often leaning in towards the other person, with a peaceful, smiling expression. This is the preferred part of the Harmonizer floor.

Emoter

The Emoter expresses the playful, creative part of the personality and is the favorite part of the Rebel type: "*Wow! Great!*" cries Joan. (Jack knits his brow), "*I'd love to work with folks like you.*" There is no malice, rancor, or ulterior motive in this part. It enables the spontaneous expression of likes and dislikes without harming anyone. It corresponds to the child part in each of us.

The tone of voice is lively and enthusiastic. Posture is open, supple, and energetic. The facial expression is radiant and expressive with twinkling eyes. Authentic feelings like grief, fear, or anger that is not blaming or attacking is also expressed through the Emoter.

Table 4.1: Personality Parts

Personality type	Most used personality part
Harmonizer	Comforter
Thinker	Computer
Persister	Computer
Imaginer	Computer
Rebel	Emoter
Promoter	Director

HOW TO GET THE MESSAGE ACROSS: COMMUNICATION CHANNELS

Communication occurs between two people when there is an offer and acceptance of that offer on the same "communication channel". Its existence proves that both personality parts are indeed compatible.

On the other hand, even if the content of the message is likely to meet the other person's approval, if delivered in an inappropriate channel it will disturb that person's perception of the content being offered. This disturbance is not related to the actual content of what is said, but usually to the way it is said. If the offer of a part is not accepted and a channel is not formed, then "miscommunication" may occur.

There are five communication channels, related to the five personality parts. Each of them is more specifically attached to one or two personality types (except for channel 1 that works like an "emergency channel").

Channel 1: Interventive

THE INTERVENTIVE CHANNEL

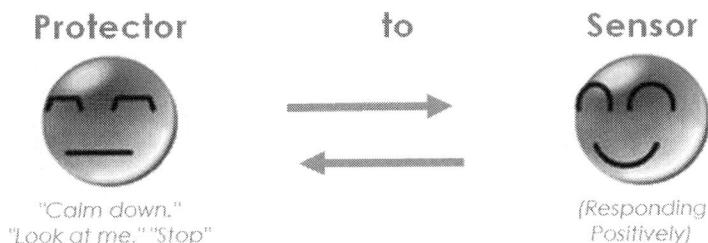

Protector   to   Sensor

"Calm down."
"Look at me." "Stop"

(Responding
Positively)

The purpose of using this channel is to intervene when communication does not occur correctly because the person is already in a situation of intense distress, overcome by emotions or confusion. It is characterized by orders in the imperative form addressed directly to the senses: touch, smell, hearing, sight, etc. The offer is from the "Protector" and should be used when an individual loses his or her self-control and a quick appropriate reaction is required or else at certain moments of the therapeutic relationship. It enables us to intervene firmly towards another person without being aggressive towards them. It should not be confused with certain injunctions: a firm "calm down" has nothing to do with the same words spoken in a brittle tone of voice. The first case is on the Interventive channel while the second is already in the field of miscommunication.

> Steven, age seven, is panicked, "It hurts. It hurts too much. I'm going to die. I'm scared." Dad takes him by the shoulders, looks him in the eye and says in a firm, soothing voice, "Calm down. Take a deep breath. Look at me". Steven, in a panicky voice: "I can't. I can't. I can't." Dad with the same calm, soothing voice: "You can breathe. Relax. Calm down." Steven slowly "comes back", is better able to control his pain, feels reassured and breathes more calmly.

> Francine bursts into her friend Brigitte's office, in total panic, "I just can't take it anymore. I'm at the end of my rope. I'm cracking up." Brigitte, in a calm, reassuring voice: "Calm down. Take a seat." Francine: "I can't it's just too much." Brigitte: "Listen to my voice, look at me me,." Francine calms down and little by little starts thinking clearly again.

These emergency and panic situations are rather exceptional, especially in the workplace. That is why the Interventive channel is rarely used. A manager can sometimes see an employee burst into the office in anger. This situation does not justify the use of this channel since the response risks coming out awkwardly with something like: "Get a grip" or "Come back when you've calmed down", which would be perceived as a refusal to communicate. It is better to answer "I see you are very angry and I am ready to hear the reasons." In this case we usually observe a return to calm.

Channel 2: Directive

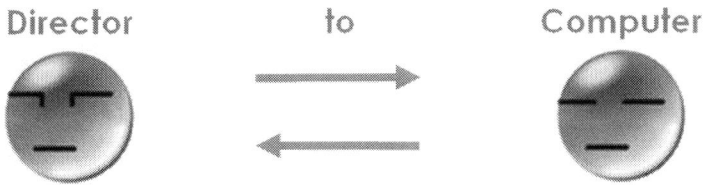

Director   to   Computer

Offer / Director: "Make a summary of this", "Tell me what your turnover is this month."
Offer acceptance / Computer: "OK", "57,000 dollars."

The response to this type of order is a piece of information delivered without any show of emotion. This channel does not aim for domination of the other person, quite the opposite. In order to be effective, the order must not contain any emotional nuance and must be received as such. To use it, we must be sure that the other's thinking part, the Computer part, is available and that the information will be received without any stress linked to feelings of guilt or frustration.

It is possible to check whether two people are communicating well on this channel by observing the quality of the response to the order. It should be clear and indicate that the person has heard the order and does not feel as if they were in an inferior-superior relationship. The answer is a bit like a computer receiving data.

Offer / Manager: "Please do this."
Manager to herself: "I'll be lucky if he does it right."
Offer non-acceptance / Employee: "I'll try." (hesitant tone)

Offer / Manager: "Please do this."
Offer acceptance / Employee: "Okay, I'll take care of it." (determined tone)

Offer / Husband: "Honey, please buy my razor blades."

Husband to himself: "Honestly, I can only count on myself."
Offer non-acceptance / Wife: "Uh, I'll try to remember."

Offer / Husband: "Honey, please buy my razor blades."
Offer acceptance / Wife: "Okay, you'll have them tonight."

People with a Promoter base prefer to use the Directive channel. They also "receive" it without any problem. Your using "kid gloves" is not important to them; what counts is having precise orders that enable them to take action while keeping their freedom of resources.

Although people with an Imaginer base do not use this channel to enter into communication, it is the channel to which they respond best. It spurs them to action. It is much less effective to use this channel with the other personality types. Still, this channel is not used very often in everyday life, since, when issuing directives, most individuals are seen to be trying to dominate the other, to make them give in, to "order them around": "Go get me some coffee. Shut the door. Be quiet". These are orders that belong to a dominant-dominated relationship and are not the use of the directive channel.

Channel 3: Requestive

THE REQUESTIVE CHANNEL

Computer   to   Computer

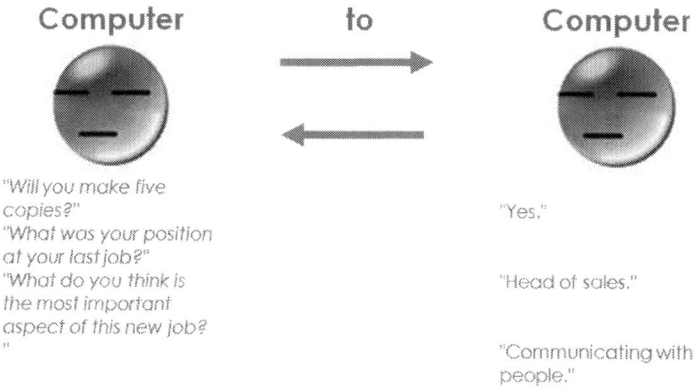

"Will you make five copies?"
"What was your position at your last job?"
"What do you think is the most important aspect of this new job?"

"Yes."

"Head of sales."

"Communicating with people."

The Requestive channel is the channel of information exchange between two people using the thinking part of their personality. We also call this "Computer-Computer", in reference to the two personality parts at play.

It works like two computers programed to exchange information.

In the workplace, the Requestive channel is one of the most important ones for the exchange of ideas and information. However, not everyone is comfortable with this type of communication. For example, people with a Harmonizer base need warm exchanges. For these people, the Requestive channel can seem dehumanized and lacking consideration.

Offer / Computer: "What position did you hold before this one?", "What is the most important aspect of your new job?", "What time is our meeting?"

Offer acceptance / Computer: "I was a supervisor", "Everything concerning the group's external communication", "At 7:00 p.m."

The Requestive channel is specific to the Thinker and Persister floors. It corresponds to their way of seeing the world and their analytical approach to problems. It is a matter of understanding for them. They analyze problems and try to break them down into simple components by comparing them to their experience in order to draw rational conclusions.

Channel 4: Nurturative

THE NURTURATIVE CHANNEL

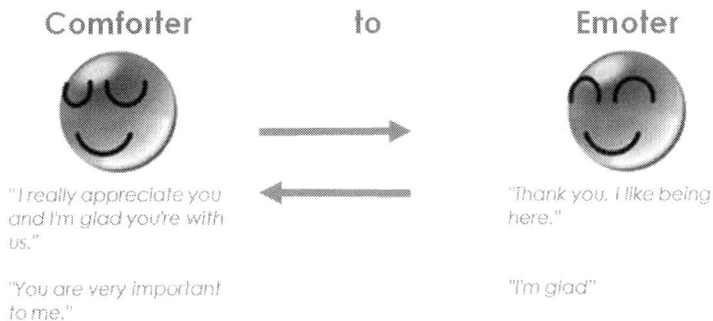

Comforter — to — Emoter

"I really appreciate you and I'm glad you're with us."

"You are very important to me."

"Thank you. I like being here."

"I'm glad"

We use this channel to convey warm messages from the Comforter part. The aim of this type of communication is to invite the other person to "feel appreciated for who they are". Managers with Thinker and Persister personality bases are usually reticent to use it because they are afraid it sounds like useless flattery. It is true that if nurturative messages are expressed insincerely, it will be instantly detected by the person being addressed. To be effective, it must be sincere and come from the heart. Naturally, this channel is very effective with Harmonizer base people. The other personality types tend to feel it is inappropriate at work.

Offer / Comforter: "I enjoy working with you. I think we do some good work in a great atmosphere."
Offer acceptance / Emoter: "Thank you. That's really nice of you!" (smiling)

Offer / Comforter: "It's so nice having you on the team.", "That's a nice tie."

Offer non-acceptance / Emoter: (silence) "Did you read the report I gave you yesterday? I think there are some essential figures in it for the rest of the project" (Thinker or Persister type answer), "What? What's wrong with my tie?" (suspicious Rebel), "Yeah, 50 bucks if you want it. So, are we going to this meeting or what?" (impatient Promoter)

Channel 5: Emotive

THE EMOTIVE CHANNEL

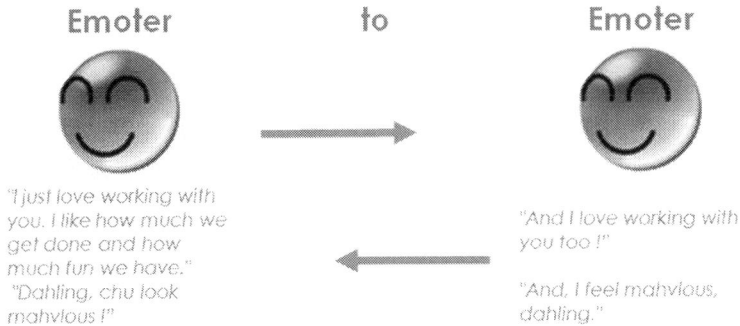

Emoter   to   Emoter

"I just love working with you. I like how much we get done and how much fun we have."
"Dahling, chu look mahvlous !"

"And I love working with you too !"

"And, I feel mahvlous, dahling."

The Emotive channel is the one on which we express our playful parts. It can help create situations in which we have fun while we work, in which a team works "on its own" in a playful mode. But this does not mean that the work does not get done. Using it in a business context does not necessarily mean "playing the clown", but simply joking a bit or being playful.

Offer / Emoter: "These photos are awesome! "This is a magic moment!"

Offer acceptance / Emoter: "They're fantastic aren't they?", "Yes! Totally intense!" (with playfulness)

The art of communication therefore consists of using the appropriate channel which will ensure that our message is accurately and effectively heard. We can begin by "practicing" communicating by using all of the personality parts, including the less familiar ones by identifying the other person's preferred communication mode. How do we do that? By listening to them, observing them, and asking questions that will enable us to quickly test the communication mode that person responds to most easily.

For instance, the "game" could be to make an offer in the four main channels and identify the one to which the response is most natural. This exercise also helps quickly memorize these different channels:

- Directive channel: "Make me a summary of the Barnes case please."
- Requestive channel: "How many files do you have to handle?"
- Nurturative channel: "If you need any help, I'm available to you if you want to talk about it."
- Emotive channel: "Wow. That is one huge pile of files."

Another example taken from a father to son encounter:

- Directive channel: "Tell me what your study plan is."
- Requestive channel: "What kind of homework do you have tonight?"
- Nurturative channel: "I'll fix you a nice snack while you do your homework."
- Emotive channel: "Wow, your exercises look fantastic!"

MANAGING THE PROCESS

When a relationship deteriorates and undercurrents begin to form, it is often due to inappropriate communication. The manager with a Thinker base believes he is making a warm compliment to his assistant when he says, "You increased your performance this month." In reality, when considered from her frame of reference, she might interpret the remark that to suggest that her boss only sees her as a machine.

What applies to the words also applies to overall demeanor. For example, when people with a Thinker or Persister base make contact, they rarely smile and focus on observing the other person in order to gather information. Vice versa, the Harmonizer base person tends to smile immediately. This type will often perceive Thinker and Persister bases as cold and this can "chill" them in turn. The Harmonizer base could even hastily conclude that they do not like her or that they do not ask questions in terms of love or personal consideration.

A young woman with a Rebel base told us how her grandfather had proven his communicating talent with her. When she was little, he was the only one able to get her to eat. Instead of suggesting "One spoon for Daddy. One spoon for Mommy", which didn't excite her at all, each time he would draw a little cartoon in the mashed potatoes. She would swallow it quickly to see the next picture. That grandfather intuitively knew how to "manage the process".

Managing the process consists in establishing a quality relationship before exchanging facts or giving instructions. To do it, we just need to use the person's preferred channel, which is what the grandfather did with his cartoons. The person's acceptance of the channel guarantees the quality of the communication to follow. Once communication is established, we can use other channels depending on the situation. Especially in the workplace, most relations require productive interactions requiring exchanges on the Requestive channel. The appropriate process enables each person to access this or verify that they are on the right channel.

You might be saying to yourself, "I don't have time to manage the process". However, what you might not notice is the time wasted in miscommunication if you don't use the process. The time spent explaining something that's "not getting across" and then being disappointed in the results and ending up doing it yourself, typically produces negative drama, waste of resources, and loss of valuable time... thinking, "The only person I can count on is myself".

> For example, a manager explains something to an employee and says, "Here is what I expect of you. Do you understand?" (The Thinker base would say, "Is it clear?" the Persister base in 1st degree distress "Have I made myself clear?").

> The person answers yes but it is sometimes a "yes" of over-adaptation to "please" or to "have some peace". In these cases, the person did not understand. She will not do what the manager expects of her. He becomes frustrated because he has wasted his time explaining and did not get the expected results. This type of situation indicates that the process was not managed, as the employee was not in Computer mode. Plus, in an attempt to be helpful, the manager will often tend to over-detail out of desire for perfection which further complicates the other person's perception of the message.

In summary, managing the process means not addressing the other person "head on" by only taking what interests *us* into consideration in *our* language. Very often we tend to expect the other person to adapt. We invite them to communicate on our own wavelength and due to this, the results are not up to our expectations.

During a supervision group[13], a participant told us:

> After the seminar, one of my very first applications was when I moved out of my office. I came in one morning while I was on vacation to pack my boxes. An employee came into the room with a file…and an urgent problem to settle. Very naturally, I turned to her and said, "I'm not here." She didn't understand. I repeated, "I'm on vacation so I'm not here." I saw a mask of frustration fall over her face. The young woman happens to have a Harmonizer base. In fact, I had sensed it but I had never clearly understood how she "ticked". When I saw her reaction, I realized I had chosen exactly the wrong response and I was able to correct my approach. Before the Process Communication Model, I would have thought, "I've screwed up again", without really knowing how or what to do about it. These are little things. Life in the workplace is made of little things like that.

In the next example, taken from a role play during a seminar, Peter, a "classic" manager, summons his Rebel base employee, Nick, to ask for an explanation.

Scene 1

> Peter – Thanks for coming in Nick. Why didn't you hand in the report? (Computer offer, Requestive channel which is not a problem at all for a Thinker base)

> Nick – Uh, the report? What report? He wrinkles his brow. He is clearly becoming distressed and starts to "try to understand". Less than a tenth of a second later, Peter's face reddens. His eyes harden, his jaw and fists clench.

---

[13] See chapter 9

Peter – Stop pretending, you know very well what I'm talking about!

His tone is brittle and does not engage a response but invites submission or resignation. Peter's heart rate has accelerated and he just wants to wring the young man's neck.

Nick – Oh! The Simpson report! (Nick answers as if he has just come back to earth). Well, it's not my fault. I wasn't able to finish it with everything they were asking me to do.

Peter – When will you finish it? (Still the same hard, brittle tone)

Nick – I don't know. I'll try to get it done as soon as possible.

Peter – I don't accept your answer. (Peter is struggling to not slam his fist on the desk). I demand to have it by tonight at the latest.

Nick – Oh, okay. I'll try.

Peter – I'll be waiting

Deep down, Peter has no illusions. There is very little chance of him obtaining the report and he can already see himself adding it to the already long list of work to do that night before presenting it to his superiors in the morning. Peter feels angry and frustrated. He feels he is not supported by his hierarchy that does not sanction people like Nick. Meanwhile, Nick has totally lost all motivation, has lost all energy for finishing the report and wonders where he could find another job.

When we study the role play, we understand that Peter attempts to communicate with Nick as if he had a Thinker base. He did not use the first three seconds of the conversation to "process manage" by responding to the need for contact (as we have seen Nick is in Rebel phase and Peter likely has had evidence of this before this interaction). As Peter was distressed, he did not perceive that his employee cannot accept Channel 3 because his need was not satisfied (when our needs are not satisfied, it is as if the elevator has broken down and we can no longer reach the upper floors). What some people might call laziness or bad faith often comes from this unsatisfied psychological need that keeps people from being motivated and efficient.

Scene 2

Peter – Hi, Nick what's up?

Nick – Dude it's a great day cuz I had a great weekend killin the tennis tourney.

Peter – Would you like some coffee? (The tone is warm and direct, Peter is open and relaxed) So, how did you "kill" the tennis tournament?

Nick answers briefly with a smile. It was awesome. Totally rocked and crushed it.

Peter – That's awesome dude! Sounds like you were in your groove. Hey, can we talk about the report?

Nick – Sure, let's do it.

In two minutes, Nick explained the situation and the reason for the late report. They looked for a solution together.

Nick – You can count on me. You'll have it on your desk by tonight.

He goes back to work. Peter takes a minute to savor the satisfaction of having solved the problem. He is sure that Nick will do a good job. Now that he is reassured, he goes back to his own task with a higher energy level.

What took place in this second version? Peter tuned into Nick's preferred channel and satisfied his need for contact. In doing so, he "energized" his staff member.

Next, he made an offer in Computer mode to see whether Nick responded on the same channel. "Can we talk about the report?" "Sure, let's do it". Nick does not show any trace of indecision or puzzlement. He is not distressed and accepts Peter's offer on the Requestive channel.

The two of them work on this channel using factual data. To conclude, Peter and Nick both feel concerned by the problem's resolution. They are in a win-win position.

Table 4.2: Using the resources of your floor

We use the resources	
Of our floor	**When**
Harmonizer	We perceive our environment through our feelings. We show authentic compassion and human warmth and we express our sensitivity. We perceive the feelings of those around us.
Thinker	We use our logic to analyze, anticipate, organize, measure and objectively treat the facts. We make a logical analysis of a situation. We seek and treat information factually.
Persister	We show devotion and conviction. We make sure our behavior corresponds to our values. We try to transmit these to our children. We "dig in" to achieve what we have decided, regardless of the difficulties we encounter.
Imaginer	We take a step back to gain perspective and better perceive situations in their entirety. We develop our visionary side by using our imagination.
Promoter	We make a decision for action, relying on our intuition without taking the time to think about it. We "instinctively" seize opportunities without assessing whether there are grounds for the decision or not.
Rebel	We express our spontaneity and creativity. We are immersed in brainstorming or throw ourselves totally into a party. We freely express our desires without worrying about how others will judge us.

With the best intentions in the world, a manager can actually express the opposite of what he or she wants to say:

> One of our trainees with a Harmonizer base had written a thick report that had required a month of work. When he showed it to a coworker with a Persister base, he heard the following: *"Thank you for asking me to read your report. Before you circulate it, I suggest you correct the mistakes that I've listed."*
>
> The author of the report thought, *"Not a word of encouragement. All he saw were the mistakes and had fun underlining them. In fact, I'm sure he looks down on me."* While his coworker thought, *"If this excellent report goes out with mistakes in it, it will be bad for my coworker's reputation and weaken the whole report. I'll do him a favor and correct it. Besides, that is what he expects of me since he asked me to read it."*

If an inappropriate channel does not automatically result in negative behavior (at least not immediately), it most certainly causes disinterest. A Promoter base person without a strong Persister floor likely is bored to death by a conversation focused on exchanging political views. On the other hand, if we talk about quick action and challenge, he opens up and feels motivated.

Table 4.3 sums up the channels to use and to avoid, depending on the other person's personality type.

Table 4.3: Choosing the Right Communication Channel

Other's personality type	Channel to use	Channel to avoid
Harmonizer	Nurturative (4)	Directive (2)
Thinker	Requestive (3)	Directive (2)
Persister	Requestive (3)	Directive (2)
Imaginer	Directive (2)	Nurturative (4)
Rebel	Emotive (5)	Directive (2)
Promoter	Directive (2)	Requestive (3)

Note: The number in parentheses indicates the communication channel number.

CHAPTER 5

THE ASSESSING MATRIX

TWO AXES AND FOUR QUADRANTS

Joan – That's all fine and dandy but how do we recognize somebody's Base? It must be cool to be able to say at first glance, "He's got a so-and-so Base, she's got a whaddya-call-it Base. Does it also work in traffic jams? You look at the driver and you go for it: I'm sure that guy's got a Thinker Base, did you see that? He looks at his watch every ten seconds. Oh, she's cool. She has a Rebel Base. Look at her, she doesn't even care. And that creep who keeps blasting his horn like a jerk, it doesn't necessarily mean he's got a Promoter Base! Hey, and look at him, did you see how he's gesticulating? He's definitely not making the sign of the cross. He looks likes he's bawling out his girlfriend as if it were her fault or else he's cussing out the police who are never there when you need them. That one over there, she's too much, she's smiling at everyone as if she liked them.

Anne – And you, what are you like in traffic jams?

Joan – It depends on the mood I'm in and what's on the radio. Either I sigh and rant or else I sing my head off as I please. Plus, I love to make fun of people, of the look on the other drivers – gently though. "Did you see that guy? If his poor mother could see him! Did you get a look at her? Looks like she's going to her boss' funeral. The guy over there is in love with himself.

Peter – Fine. Very good. If you keep on, you'll go through your entire repertoire. What were we supposed to discuss? How to identify the Base? Let's go over our course; who understands what the Assessing Matrix is?

Jack – I think I've integrated the concept. It is a two-axis matrix. The vertical axis corresponds to the motivation axis.

Joan – The what axis?

Jack – Motivation. I'm speaking English, aren't I?

Joan – You're always so much fun.

Jack – If you say so. So, as I was saying, the motivation axis, I mean the vertical axis has two poles.

Joan – Yeah, north and south I bet. (Smiling, she watches for Jack's reaction out of the corner of her eye).

Jack – Love it. Let's go for north and south. In the north, we find people who are internally motivated and tend to initiate contact with others.

Isabelle – Oh, I can see myself in that. I'm always the one who starts by saying hello and I'm usually surprised to see myself smiling at people I don't even know.

Joan – You see, that's what I was talking about before with the traffic jams.

Jack – Let's focus. So, I said people in the north tend to initiate contact, like you Isabelle, and vice versa, those from the south…

Joan – They've all gone south!

Jack – Yes, in the south, like you, they react to external stimulation.

Joan – It's true, that sometimes I really think you look like an external stimulation.

(Jack, wrinkles his brow with an automatic glance at the clock).

Isabelle – Okay, Joan, be nice and let him finish. Look how hard he's trying to explain it to us.

Joan – I promise, I'll pipe down. Go ahead Jack, give us the big north-south divide.

Jack – In the north we speak of "internal trigger" and in the south of "external trigger". Joan, do you want to tell us how you answer a salesperson in a store who asks what you're looking for?

Joan – With me it's always on impulse. Sometimes the look on the salesperson's face makes me laugh.

Jack – The impulse tells us that your buying motivation will be invited by the item you see.

Peter – That's interesting because I'm the other way around. I walk into a store with a precise idea in mind of what I'm looking for and if I don't find it I go someplace else. I'm totally oblivious to a salesperson who might try to sell something other than what I came for.

Jack – Thank you for these two contributions. Joan, your motivation would be activated by the outside, so we say "external trigger", the south pole. While Peter, your motivation is internal. You know what you are looking for, so we speak of "internal trigger" – the north pole, to use Joan's image.

Joan – I'm starting to get it. Don't you have a story to illustrate it?

Jack – (thinks a second) When I was a young engineer…

Joan – A long time ago!

Jack – External trigger. Do you understand?

(Joan smiles)

Jack – I was with a coworker one Friday night and our boss told us, "Guys, you've done a great job. Next week is break time. You both get a week off.

Joan – Cool boss!

Jack – I immediately knew what I was going to do. I had promised myself I would go hiking in Ireland the first chance I got. My coworker didn't say anything. He thanked our boss and he was absorbed in thought when we left the office. We took the subway together and at 59th street he suddenly cried, "That's where I want to go. He pointed to poster with a breathtaking view of the Aegean Sea."

Joan – I could kiss you. I just understood my "love it or hate it" temperament people sometimes criticize me for.

Jack – To summarize, some people will take the initiative to enter into contact with others. We can say they are self-motivated. In other words, their motivation is caused by an internal trigger. Others are motivated by an external trigger and tend not to initiate contact.

Joan – So, for me, when I walk into the office and ask you, "What's bugging you this morning?" What's the trigger? I talk and everybody else sulks?

Jack – Of course not, dear Joan.

Joan – I love it when you speak to me like that.

Jack – It is the external trigger because it's "our look" that invites your reaction.

Joan – Wow, now I get it. Isabelle, you enter the office and it's like you were giving us each a kiss just in the way you lick us with your, "Hi everyone".

Isabelle – Lick?

Joan – Yeah, like a big wet lick of affection.

Isabelle – (slightly miffed) – Okay, if you say so…

Tom – Okay, let's get at it! Show us how it works, Jack.

(Jack stands up, chooses three different colored markers to draw the matrix. He traces a vertical axis and a horizontal axis).

Jack – The vertical axis is the goal axis. In the north, representing the internal triggers, people initiate contact. The horizontal axis is the relationship axis. Two poles. East and west, Joan?

Joan – If you say so…

Jack – In the west we find people who enjoy being in groups or a part of group efforts. We say that they are "involving" on the relationship axis. To the east we find people who prefer to be alone or with only one other person. For these people, we say that they are "withdrawing" on the relationship axis. Now, I'll position the six personality types on the four quadrants.

Figure 5.1: Assessing matrix

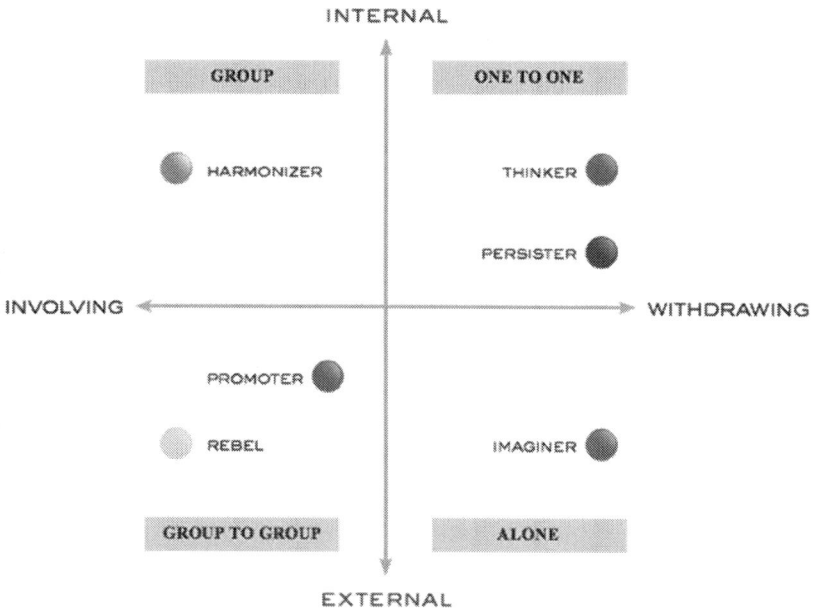

Peter – I can't agree with that. You put the Persister type towards the "Withdrawing" pole when I'm an extremely involved person.

Joan – Yeah, right. You're really involved in your beliefs but when you ask me how I'm doing I'd be surprised if it really interested you. While our gentle Isabelle asks for more. In fact, speaking of our Isabelle, if by chance she is in conflict with someone, she's sad and has trouble working. While, Peter, you don't care if you're in conflict with someone. You don't seem the least bit affected by it.

Peter – Being in conflict with someone means defending your ideas, that's what counts.

Jack – Yes, exactly, that's why we say "withdrawing" because in your example, the priority isn't the quality of the relationship but the nature of the debate. Here's another example: one of us, whose name I won't mention (a wink at Joan), often criticizes me for what she calls my "get to the point" side.

Joan – That's the least we can say with your clipped attitude. If, for instance, I tell you your tie couldn't be tackier. And then your "What do you want?" comes straight out of the freezer. It's no surprise we sometimes catch cold!

Jack – I love your reaction.

Joan – So you're giving us a little foray into the involving side?

Jack – If I want to proceed, I have to adapt.

Tom – Nice ping-pong match people. I'm more about action. Explain to me why you put me on the "external trigger" side.

Jack – The Promoter type takes action after external stimulation. Remember the ad campaign "Put a tiger in your tank?" That's a perfectly Promoter headline.

Tom – It's true. I need something to happen to get in gear. I remember when I bought my first BMW. I had seen a gorgeous picture, in an awesome setting. The car was magnificent, the driver was alone and the headline read, "Men haven't finished loving cars". I got an immediate adrenaline rush and thought, "I want one like that". That very evening I had an appointment at the BMW dealership.

Joan – Struttin' your little stuff again.

Tom – Why little?

Joan – Smooth!

PREFERRED ENVIRONMENT

Quadrant 1: Internal Trigger – Involving in the Relationship

People with a Harmonizer Base seek groups as long as their atmosphere is pleasant. Remember that these people dislike conflict and usually try to avoid it. If they work in an open space, they regularly renew their energy by a mere look or nod from their coworkers. They especially like a smile or a wink that makes them feel close. Coffee breaks give them a chance to experience warm, even intimate moments and provide an excellent opportunity for them to recharge their batteries.

Isabelle – I especially like Wednesday mornings when I look forward to us all getting together for our monthly meeting, and the idea of starting our meeting with fifteen minutes of emotion. It helps us strengthen our ties with each other every time.

Tom – It's true that when we started this rite of fifteen minutes of emotion, I thought we'd all turned into boy scouts. Now I would miss it if we eliminated our jump-start routine!

Jack – Did you noticed that our dear Isabelle always finds something to say to everyone, telling us how important we are to her?

Anne – Sometimes I think I'd like to be able to do that.

Joan – Take your elevator instead of star gazing.

Anne – I'll consider it.

Jack – Let's begin with our agenda now.

Joan – Attention Ladies and Gentlemen, get ready for take-off!

Harmonizer Base – First Contact

People with a Harmonizer Base usually take the initiative to make contact, if only non-verbally. This Personality Type is usually smiling and first seeks to establish a personal relationship with others by taking an authentic interest in them. The content of their conversation is oriented more towards personal life rather than business: "Where are you from?", "Do you have any children?" This natural mode of making contact aims to receive a positive answer to their existential question, "Am I loveable?"

Quadrant 2: Internal Trigger / Withdrawing in the Relationship – Task-Oriented

People with a Thinker or Persister Base fall into this quadrant. They usually prefer to work alone on projects or with just one other person. Their concern is efficiency and they usually find the individual relationship more appropriate than the group one.

They take the initiative to make contact depending on their objective: getting to know someone, seeking information, discovering the other person's opinions, etc.

Jack – It's logical. We're a lot more efficient working alone. There is no time wasted and a relationship with just one person helps us get straight to the point.

Peter – I don't entirely agree. Being with a group helps get the same message across to each person.

Jack – Do you hear what you are saying? You said "being with a group" instead of "in a group". If I understand you, it is a matter of conveying your message rather than dialoguing with each person. So you don't seek the relationship, you seek efficiency.

Peter – True, I agree.

Joan – Oh boy! Aren't you splitting hairs just a tad?

We can note that the Persister type is close to quadrant 3, the Imaginer type. Many people with a Persister Base are also comfortable with the energy of the Imaginer type.

Another point: we can note that they tend less to initiate contact than the Thinker type. The reason for this is that they wait to form an opinion before speaking.

Peter – I am totally convinced of that point. For me, it's essential to speak purposefully in order to know who I am dealing with and what it's all about. I recently took a training course. Halfway through, the trainer asked my opinion about it. I thought the question was a bit strange because I couldn't have a definite idea of the course until it was finished.

Thinker Base: First Contact

We can identify a Thinker Base in another person by their natural tendency to deliver information – sometimes even too much information.

People of this type attach importance to showing us their competency and often refer to their experience and/or achievements as an attempt to positively answer their existential question "Am I competent?"

Among their concerns is the relationship with time and they demonstrate their desire to optimize it by striving for flawless punctuality and expect the same from others.

Tom – I pulled off a nice one when I asked a prospect how much time he had for my demonstration. He almost unwillingly allotted me 45 minutes. I worked it so I finished in 43 minutes. When I said goodbye I looked at my watch and said soberly but with a wink, "two minutes saved". I saw gratefulness and relief in his eyes. I'm sure he sees me as a real pro.

Joan – Better change your hat.

Tom – Huh?

Joan – To fit over that big head!

Persister Base – First Contact

Relational dynamics in people with a Persister Base are based on trust. "Am I trustworthy?" is their existential question. "Can I give my trust?" is a question they often ask themselves.

When we first make contact, the person weighs us and tries to assess our degree of sincerity. Looking at a person with this Base Personality Type in the eye is very important for inspiring trust.

One manager told us, "I usually form my opinion in three seconds: either they're above board or they're not".

In a sales situation, an overly eager salesperson is doomed to fail with a Persister prospect. Our Persister prospects need time to accord their trust. Once it is acquired, this Personality Type can be our best ambassadors: "You can trust her", "He knows what he's doing", "He's a straight arrow".

We can strengthen our first impression of a person with a Persister Base by listening to his or her opinions. Sincere rewording is a powerful tool for satisfying the needs for recognition of work and conviction. It means, *"Your opinion is important to me"* followed by *"I have understood you"*.

"I'm warning you, you're in competition," said a business school director in a vaguely threatening tone during a selection interview. The interview lasted exactly one hour during which the director told

us about the school, its values, and of his vision and strong opinions on how to train business managers. We listened to him, intervening occasionally in the form of questions-rewording. At the end of the interview he asked us, "Have you been given the dates and times for the intervention?", "I imagine you will send it to me if our proposal is selected," we answered. "I've made my decision. It's you".

Quandrant 3: External Trigger / Withdrawing in the Relationship – Task-Oriented

Joan – Can you tell us about the first contact or lack of contact?

Anne – I wait for people to approach me; sometimes I see them reach out to me when it isn't even true.

Jack – I think this is a perfect illustration of the existential question for the Imaginer personality type.

Joan – I sometimes think you are a perfect illustration of the Encyclopedia personality type. It doesn't exist? Oh, well we'll have to invent one just for you.

Imaginer Base: First Contact

On first contact, people with an Imaginer Base can often seem distant, absent, or uninterested.

Isabelle – I often feel uncomfortable with those people because I feel like they don't like me.

Joan (to Jack) – Hey, can you do your existential question number again?

Jack – They didn't spank you enough when you were a kid.

Joan – If you say so.

During interviews, we should take care to guide this person by being brief, concise, and straightforward and by accepting the need for time to develop his views. We will obtain rich, deep responses if we give it time.

Anne (after a moment of thought) – Yes, for me, it's like a groundswell that takes a long time to rise to the surface and that I have to nurture in order to reap its fruits.

Joan – Fruits from a wave… you know you're a bit of a poet Anne?

Anne answers with a smile.

Quadrant 4: External Trigger / Involving in the Relationship

Promoter Base: First Contact

People with a Promoter Base usually use an external stimulus to enter into contact. Noting a prospect's new car: "It looks like business is booming". Discreetly referring to a prospect's jacket label: "I dress at Boss, too". With a knowing smile: "That tan in the middle of winter – the Caribbean?"

This profile often gives the impression of wanting to direct the discussion while still agreeing with everything we say. They know how to "stroke the other's ego" and can at times slightly overplay what is expected: "You are entirely right about that. It's the least we can do, and if you allow me, I'd just like to add that…"

Tom – I would just like to add that you hit it on the head. The art of hooking people and away we go!

Peter – It is important to remain vigilant to the difference between influence and manipulation.

Tom – Oh yeah? And do you see a difference between them? What counts are the results, right?

Peter – In-te-gri-ty. That's the whole difference that makes…a difference.

Joan – I love your new tag line: "Peter, integrity makes a difference". You oughta get it trademarked!

(Peter clears his throat and says nothing)

Tom – "With integrity, your results will skyrocket". That one's not bad either!

Jack – Let's get back to our topic.

Rebel Base: First Contact

Just like the people with a Promoter Base, people with a Rebel Base will enter into contact through external stimulation. They react. "I want to" or "I don't want to" are usually the behavioral triggers. The difference between these two Personality Types is that, for one of them, the goal is what counts, the finality: "I'm definitely not leaving until he signs". For the other, it is the reaction: "I want to be in contact with that person or not on the basis of the reaction". For the Rebel type, they are much more focused on the here and now than the Promoter type.

Joan – I hate it when I see through other people. For example, you Tom, when you come to see me with your Joan-baby-you-look-hot-in-your-new-top number, I could puke!

Tom – (with a knowing wink) – Are you sure you're not interested?
Joan – You're a hoot, you know that?

Table 5.2: Preferred Environment by Personality Type

Harmonizer	Often initiate contact by trying to establish a personal relationship.
Thinker	Easily initiate contact by trying to establish an intellectual or professional discussion.
Persister	Usually take the time to form an opinion before speaking. First assess the interest in entering into contact with their environment.
Imaginer	Are not usually involved, provide brief responses to verbal solicitation from others.
Promoter	Use stimuli related to the other person to enter into contact and often try to interact to achieve their goals.
Rebel	Enter into contact if the other person appeals to them and if they want to. Do not usually use "kid gloves" to make their intentions known.

A STIMULATION TRIGGER

To conclude this chapter on motivational triggers, we asked senior manager Erik, age 44, for permission to publish his very compelling story that says it all. Eric has a Thinker Base and Phase.

When I was very young (age 7) I was very good in school and attended a private Catholic institution. I was advanced in terms of both knowledge and maturity. The Nuns that ran the school called me the Encyclopedia and they even changed the rules such that I could be in first male student to attend their all-girl school. In other words, no one doubted my future scholastic success (except for me as I didn't realize it).

My great-grandfather was a tremendous moral standard for the entire family and for me. This man, a demi-god in my eyes, began saying, "This boy will attend a military academy". But other than knowing that he thought that attending a military academy was the ultimate pinnacle, I didn't know the full extent of what a military academy was (I don't think he did either). Those words, repeated without any pressure and echoed by the rest of the family, sounded more like a prophecy than an order. Those words left their mark on me and, in a way, made me who I am.

My great-grandfather died when I was 11 and his words became even more magical because they mingled with the memories of a man who, 33 years later, still brings tears to my eyes whenever he is mentioned. I owed him my loyalty.

So until my last year of high school, when my friends asked me what I was going to do later, I answered "I'm going to a military academy". They chuckled, but not so much due to my grades (which were sufficient), as due to the fact that everyone else answered with a job or an adventure or another story, while I just answered with that single statement. Two months before prep school was to start, I was unaware that I would have to attend it in order to pass the academy's entrance exam. Admittedly, my family had stopped repeating the prophecy since the death of my great-grandfather.

Ultimately I was accepted into prep school. I was told which curriculum I should take to attend the academy, which I took without question, and was ultimately deemed "admissible to the entrance exam". When I went for my oral exam I was awed by the beauty of the campus. I failed the exam that year without knowing anything more about the school except that I had seen it and could visualize it. The following year passed without my learning any more about the academy but with the peaceful certainty that the goal was achievable. I achieved it as I passed the entrance exam a year later.

When I found out I had been accepted, I did not feel any joy (unlike my family whose reaction could fill a book). I spent my vacation peacefully storing away my past to prepare for this future that had always been mine.

I boarded a train with a ticket paid for by the army and traveled to the base. From that point on, everything started to fall apart. The train stunk, my arrival was a bumpy ride in a rattling old bus, and I was welcomed by military officers who that very afternoon had me crawling in a muddy trench before sending me to boot camp and then reserve officer's school and ultimately my regiment. All of my classmates knew about this phase (which wasn't really as bad as that but which I experienced as traumatic). They had no problem with it and I just didn't understand a thing.

It is interesting to consider here why I didn't understand a thing. My goal was to attend a military academy. I didn't accurately define "military", as I had imagined. it as a paradise of science and knowledge that was merely "dressed" in military garb.

That year the military taught me a lot (perhaps it is what formed me the most) but it was a year of suffering due to the upheaval it caused me. I ultimately attended the school for 2 years but something was broken. I was never again able to study like I had formerly. In fact, I had achieved the goal and found myself facing a multi-faceted void:

First facet: And now, what can I do concretely?

Second facet: Why did I do this instead of something else?

Third facet: I fell apart emotionally and had to rebuild myself entirely.

At the end of the second year, I had to fill in the options sheet for the remainder of my studies. I had just returned from a 3-month internship in Sweden and the world had changed. All of my classmates were already settled in the future (some engaged, others interning in their future companies, others working on the curricula for the following years). And I still felt the same void ahead of me and a wish-list to fill out for the next day.

So I called my father. He advised me to choose the weapons corps with an aeronautics option because, as a scientist, he had seen the resources in that department and the weaponry engineers who worked there. So I chose the weapons corps, more by default than by fondness. I do not regret anything. In my 20 year career and personal life, I have more or less filled the void. As I approached the age of 44, I now work in a totally different capacity where I am much more my own motivational trigger. I know what I am going to do now and it has taken me 44 years to visualize it and prepare for it.

CHAPTER 6

MISCOMMUNICATION

"There was a misunderstanding, and if you know anything about the world, this will not surprise you in the least." Albert Camus

In interpersonal communication situations, conversations can go well or degrade very quickly. Dr. Taibi Kahler chose the word "miscommunication" to refer to the phenomena of incomprehension, conflict, or passivity that we encounter frequently. He also observed that in many cases, miscommunication was due to the failure to use the right Perception and Channel. This invited the first stage of distress which, if not addressed, could lead to deeper distress.

EFFECTS OF DISTRESS

All individuals stop thinking clearly when in distress. Our ability to solve problems is altered and, entirely unconsciously, we tend to see things the way we believe they are instead of the way they actually are.

If we are in contact with another person and distress occurs, the conversation will become non-productive as it may only be distantly related to the apparent purpose of the conversation. That is why we call it miscommunication.

When miscommunication is occurring and someone is in distress, we describe them as "wearing a mask." We describe it this way because the distressed behavior hides the person's normal productive self, much as a mask hides the face of the person wearing it. "Masks" are identifiable by a transformation in facial expressions. For example, eyes darken, wrinkles are accentuated, the face becomes painful or stony. Each time we observe a mask on another person, we can deduce that the person is becoming distressed and that, if this stress increases, the person will think less and less clearly, responding with unconscious unproductive behavior. Example:

A – Can you explain the reasons why...

B – Okay, enough already! In fact, I know very well what you're trying to say. You think it's my fault if...

B is distressed. He is convinced that A is trying to trap him and will probably try to verify this belief without realizing that A is simply seeking information.

Another characteristic of distressed behavior is that masks invite masks from others. Why? Because the spontaneous responses to masked behavior are fight or flight. In other words, another masked behavior whose purpose is protection from the masked person. Let's take an example:

Jack begins, "I should explain how Drivers are an important component, an essential component to understand in both communication and miscommunication". Jack (Thinker Base) is over-detailing slightly and Joan (Rebel Base) wrinkles her brow, "How?" Jack continues, "Yes, I said (repeats the information). Do you follow me?" "Well, um, not really..." Jack starts again but his impatience is growing. His slightly masked behavior has "clashed" with Joan's mask.

Another example:

Isabelle (Harmonizer Base) addresses Tom (Promoter Base): "Is everything okay? You don't need anything?" "No thank you", answers Tom in a gruff voice, barely raising his eyes from his page.

This gruff voice invites Isabelle to feel unrecognized. Without realizing it, she might even insist in order to obtain recognition or she may "sulk". Tom could get angry without understanding that he really did not put much energy into the relationship that Isabelle was seeking.

It is very important to be watchful for the first indicative signs and the first mask. As soon as the process turns towards miscommunication, content will have difficulty getting across. In this case, in order to return to a positive discussion, we must decode the meaning of the behavior by responding positively. Knowledge of the personality types, their respective psychological needs and the use of their preferred perceptions and preferred communication channels are three tools that serve this goal.

Dr. Taibi Kahler identified three degrees of miscommunication. The first one, the Driver, is the "doorway". The second one is characterized by wearing the Attacker, Blamer or Drooper masks and activating certain predictable failure mechanisms. The third degree is the Despairer mask (Figure 6.1).

FIRST DEGREE OF MISCOMMUNICATION: DRIVERS

As the "doorway" to miscommunication, drivers are subtle behaviors that are difficult to perceive. They act as warning signals to indicate that the person is becoming distressed. Drivers are unconscious, unemotional defense mechanisms. The essential problem these drivers pose is the risk of entering second degree distress in which the person will experience harmful energy that activates their failure mechanisms (see below).

There are five main drivers: Please, Try Hard, Be Strong, Be Perfect, and Hurry Up. Each personality type uses one of them, except for the Hurry Up driver which is not specific to any one personality type.

Figure 6.1: Miscommunication Occurs When One of the People Wears a Mask

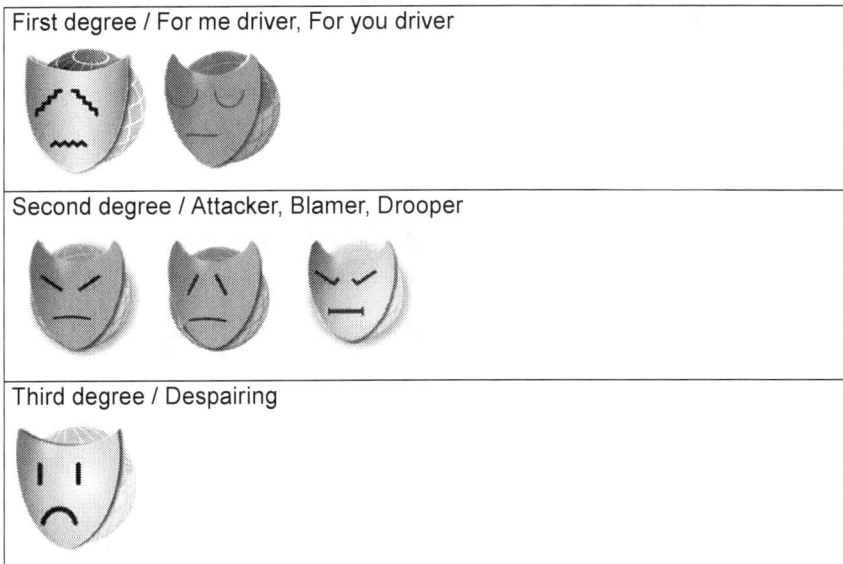

First degree / For me driver, For you driver

Second degree / Attacker, Blamer, Drooper

Third degree / Despairing

Harmonizer Type Driver: Please You

Fred is an adorable 4 year-old boy. He is angry and Mom probably won't like it and will send him to his room. "You can come back when you're a good boy again" she will say. He discovers when he activates his driver "Please you", then his mother's attitude changes entirely. Conclusion: he'll reinforce his driver when discovering he has every interest in pleasing and focuses more on people's satisfaction than on what he feels himself.

For example, adults ask him to eat a little more meat "for Daddy" and some vegetables for "Grandma". Without driver, he could have thought it's strange to do it for them rather than because he is hungry, but he obeys. By repeating this type of behavior, he learns that it is the most efficient way of obtaining positive attention when he needs it.

A few years later…

Fred has grown up now and graduated from catering school, which suits his Harmonizer base. People with a Harmonizer base love anything having to do with food in particular and enjoy sharing this pleasure. Fred works in a big restaurant. He is a pleasant person: wide smile, spontaneous, attentive to the customers' needs. But he has recently encountered some difficulties. The restaurant has decided to cater to a clientele of business people who seldom show signs of recognition of person. Fred explains, "I don't feel good with my clientele anymore. The people aren't very nice; they're not very friendly. I just don't feel recognized, when up until now, everyone smiled at me and called me by my first name. Now, I barely get a thank-you – and that's on a good day!"

Characteristic Behavior of the Please You Driver

In the first degree of distress, Fred tends to not ask for what he wants directly. He will say things like, "Maybe I could take a day off?", "Perhaps I could leave a little early?", "It's not important. As you wish." He has difficulty saying no.

The constraining Please you driver makes it difficult for people to make decisions and they are uncomfortable when someone around them is displeased. That is why managers with a Harmonizer base run their teams by seeking a consensus and are attached to creating a pleasant atmosphere. Since they are uncomfortable with conflict, they put energy into avoiding it or into trying to resolve it as soon as it appears.

Imaginer Type Driver: Be Strong for You

If Sebastian cries because he fell down and scraped his knee, he is looked down on by his father or big brother who say, "Men don't cry". Sebastian will continue to reinforce his Be Strong for you Driver. He no longer expresses his feelings and desires. "Be quiet," he is told, "It doesn't hurt"; when he knows very well that it hurts.

A few years later…

Sebastian is now 27. He is usually described as a loner and a bit reserved. He never expresses his feelings. He loves to pump iron. People describe him as being as "a trooper". He is a huge fan of bicycle racing, especially the grueling, mid-winter, middle of the night variety. His main difficulty? He is unable to become attached to anyone.

He works at a service station but only handles the register now that the pumps are automatic. He likes that his job doesn't require too much concentration and he has little contact with others. He is never sick and figures things out for himself when he has a problem. He tries to convince himself that "a real pro doesn't need anyone".

Characteristic Behavior of the Be Strong for you Driver

Sebastian's behavior at the gym where he works out is always the same. He arrives, waves to the employee and then sets to work on the machines by himself. He makes no contact and doesn't speak to anyone. Others customers joke about him in small groups as they move around the machines. He barely seems to notice them. When he is finished, he showers, dresses, and leaves with the same wave on the way out. When something is wrong, it is as if his face were closed. He becomes less expressive than usual, as if he wasn't there. One of the characteristic signs of the Be Strong for you driver is to "crawl into his shell". At family reunions or long, loud meetings, it is not rare for Sebastian to wear an absent look, gazing into space, absorbed in his inner life. We can say that the Be Strong for you driver signals a curfew: it's time to crawl into his shell to avoid relational overstimulation.

Thinker Type Driver: Be Perfect for You

Bert doesn't like to work at school. Not at all. He is bored there. Of course, his grades show it. When he shows his parents, his father doesn't say anything and simply turns away from him. But the other day, without quite knowing how, he got an A in math. It was the first time. When he announced the extraordinary results to his father, his Dad hugged him and told him he how proud he was of him. Bert reinforced his Be Perfect for you by thinking that getting good grades in school enabled him to get lots of attention from his father. To gain attention, he had to be perfect.

A few years later…

Bert is 35. He is an excellent handyman. As he explains, "It's incredible. The whole room is impeccable. I bought some beautiful, very expensive wallpaper and carefully calculated my rolls but I realized I didn't have enough to finish a totally invisible corner inside the closet. Can you believe it? I had to buy another whole roll! At the same time I was annoyed because I thought it was stupid to spend so much on something no one would ever see. Yet, if I didn't I wouldn't feel as if I had finished."

Bert feels he is not allowed to make mistakes. He would have preferred to hide the mistake instead of admitting to it or hear his boss tell him he had made a mistake, that he wasn't "perfect".

Characteristic Behavior of the Be Perfect for You Driver

Under the influence of his driver, Bert over-explains and makes unnecessary qualifications in statements for a long time before choosing exactly the right words to express his thoughts. As a manager, he can have difficulty delegating. He believes he can do tasks better and faster than the others. And he even goes so far as to say, "They're less competent. That's why I have to do it myself." And his staff will think, "There's no need to really bother since he redoes everything after us anyway."

Rebel Type Driver: Try Hard for You

As a toddler, when Julie began eating on her own, her mother did not like to see her paint the room with yogurt and mashed veggies, or spend so much time swallowing three carrots that had escaped her creativity. But if her mom intervened to help her daughter finish her meal, if she did it *for* her, the atmosphere immediately relaxed. Julie very quickly reinforced her Try Hard for you driver by trying to do something but not actually do it herself. As soon as things become difficult, Julie needs to feel that someone is taking care of her because she can't do it by herself. "I don't understand," she says as she tries hard.

A few years later…

Today Julie is an IT correspondent for a big multi-national company. She loves her job which enables her to play with her computer and be in contact with lots of people. It is also her job to make the connection between accounting and IT. Since the IT department is filled with people who have the same profile as herself, this gives her an opportunity to spend a pleasant moment with her colleagues. Her boss has a Persister base and is in a Thinker phase. He tends to give her instructions using the Requestive channel: clear, straightforward and efficient with no chit-chat. This is when Julie wrinkles her brow, stops thinking clearly and doesn't understand anymore. She displays a struggling expression on her face and says, "Huh? What?" which seriously annoys her boss.

Characteristic Behavior of the Try Hard for You Driver

When she was a teen, Julie would often say, "Boy am I fed up. Math is too hard. I just don't get it. I'll never be able to do this" or, with a sigh, "This is giving me a headache",

A person with a Rebel base in first degree distress can react like this to a direct question:

- What do you do for a living?
   o Huh?

- I'd like to know what your job is.
   o And what do you want to know?

- What is your job?
   o But when you say my job, it's…

- Well, your occupation.

We can identify this driver by its laborious aspect, by phrases punctuated with "um" and "how can I put it". It is as if the thought will just not "come out".

For you Drivers – For me Drivers

The four drivers we have just seen are "for you" drivers. In other words, they express the following life position: "You are OK, I would be OK if". It is a "conditional +", meaning, "I am OK on the condition that I please you, on the condition that I try hard, etc." If a person is unable to fulfill this "condition", they are not OK (an excellent personal indicator for identifying our own drivers):

- Harmonizer type: I must please you. If I say no to someone, I'm not OK at having displeased them.
- Thinker type: I must be perfect for you. I'm not OK if I leave the office before finishing a task.
- Rebel type: I must try hard for you. I'm not OK If I don't try hard. I am spending a lot of energy and getting nowhere.
- Imaginer type: I must be strong for you. I'm not OK if I express my feelings. I unconsciously think that, anyway, I am alone and can only count on myself.

The person is not OK if their inner demands of right perception and right channel are not met.

The two remaining personality types, the Persister and Promoter, will show For me Drivers which are Be Perfect for me and Be Strong for me. Their life position is the following: "I'm OK, you would be OK if…" What they demand of themselves they also demand of others and will let them know it.

Promoter Type Driver: Be Strong for Me

Julian is a boy who manages by himself. His parents believed this would arm him to face life. From birth, he acts as if he needs to be strong to survive and adapt to a sometimes unfriendly environment. He learned early how to recognize "good" people, in other words, "strong" people. This is what we call the Be Strong for me driver. Under the influence of this driver, the person will not only demand strength and independence of themselves, but also of others.

A few years later…

Julian heads a sales team. He can't stand "dependents", which explains his difficulties with employees with a Harmonizer base who are always trying to please him in hopes of getting a little personal attention in return. Julian sees these emotional demonstrations as particularly inappropriate and tends to, as he puts it, "send packing" anyone demonstrating "emotional overflow".

Characteristic Behavior of the Be Strong for Me Driver

Typical phrases from Julian are messages based on, "Figure it out without me", "You just have to read the instructions". A manager under the influence of the Be Strong for me driver establishes relationships involving challenges with others. Julian tends to manage his team with an "each man for himself" approach and does not provide support to his team members who need it. "Listen to me, I pulled myself up by my bootstraps, I didn't need anybody's help, so don't count on me to be your babysitter. There are no lame ducks on my team." A typical expression for a Promoter profile would be, "We only have *real* men here", and turning to the women, "And girls, if you're on my team, it's because you can do like the guys."

In another style, a charming elderly woman of 84 years of age, unwittingly gave us an illustration of a "wonderful" Be Strong for me driver. Her life had been a series of adventures and inconceivable risks for a woman of her time. When we asked her to tell us what her fears were, she calmly considered us and replied, "Fear? But I was never afraid. I don't know what that is. I have not felt fear since childhood. When I was little, my father used to send me into the back yard late at night in the dark to get his tools. I was very frightened but I never said so. My father would say, 'That's good, you're strong. You are both the girl and the boy I wanted, you're both at the same time. I'm proud of you.' I reinforced that to be loved, I needed to be strong."

Persister Type Driver: Be Perfect for Me

When she was small, Laura already believed that she had a role to play in keeping people responsible and serious. She was like a child who grew up too fast. At age seven, when she played with her dolls, she would often lecture them in a very parental tone. As a teen, she demanded that her little sister be toilet trained, eat all her food, etc. In other words, she was already playing the mother and pressuring her sister to be perfect.

A few years later...

Laura heads an intensive care ward in a large medical clinic. She is seen as someone cold and very demanding. Someone who doesn't smile. The nurse whose base is Rebel regularly says, "Scramble everybody, here comes the cop." Things must be done the way *she* wants them. She has a very high opinion of her job and how things should be run in a healthcare environment.

Characteristic Behavior of the Be Perfect for Me Driver

"I would like you to summarize the essential values you find in this model by considering both the work that has been done, your concrete experience, your background and of course your previous training. I'm listening." For Laura this is a natural way of expressing herself. Audience perceptions: one person's eyes blur, another has already decided she's hearing a foreign language, the third has pushed his inner computer into overdrive, the fourth readily absorbs the information and prepares to address it, and the fifth has already forgotten what was requested!

Another characteristic of the Be Perfect for me driver is asking three questions at once as well as a tendency to focus on what is wrong instead of what is right.

"There's no need to tell the staff they are doing their jobs well. It's the least they can do. That's what they're paid for. On the other hand, we can't tolerate the least mistake or else where will we end up?"

This type of behavior causes reactions among the staff like, "My boss never tells me what's good but there's always some little thing that's wrong and he always nails me about it."

A family story to illustrate this Be Perfect for me driver: It's report card day. Dad has a Persister base, his son is a Thinker base. Dad sees that his son received all A's and one B on his report card. He doesn't say anything about the A's but points to the B and says, "Son, what's the problem?"

Another scene from marital life this time: A wife has gone to a lot of trouble to prepare a delicious meal. "Is it good, honey?" she asks her husband in hopes of receiving attention. Absorbed in his concerns at work, the husband answers; "As long as I don't say anything, it means it's good."

If we listen carefully to Laura, we realize that she words many sentences negatively. "That's not a bad piece of work you've done" (meaning "good work"), "what you just said is not of the slightest importance" (meaning "that's a good idea"), "This meal isn't bad", etc. She (sometimes regretfully) concludes that "there's nothing to say", meaning the work that was delivered is perfect.

One Driver Does It, Two Overdoes It

We have seen that the drivers act as a "doorway" to the miscommunication process. Their appearance is extremely brief and quick and can occur dozens of times in ordinary conversations. Several drivers can succeed one another in the same sentence. Even if we mainly show the driver corresponding to our base, we can also show the driver corresponding to our phase or to our stage. "*If you want* (Please you), *at this stage, I would like* (Be Perfect for you)." Or, for instance, "*I mean, well, I would very much like it if, um, how can I put it, um, to* (Try Hard) *give you a clear, concrete, precise, verifiable example* (Be Perfect for you)."

But real difficulties will begin if the person moves into second degree miscommunication. Being attentive to the drivers delivers precious information in terms of perception and channel of communication to use and helps us avoid distress "escalation." Below is an example of everyday dialogue that is rich in drivers.

> Isabelle and Peter are leaving on a business trip together on Saturday morning. Isabelle calls Peter to decide where to meet. Peter has just come back from a difficult meeting. He is distressed. Fortunately, both of them are familiar with Process Communication Model.
>
> Isabelle is experiencing Please you Driver, when Peter is experiencing Be Perfect for you driver.
>
> Isabelle – Can I ask a little question? If I don't bother you, I have a very heavy suitcase. Could you maybe stop by here and pick me up? (They live not far from one another)

Peter (clipped tone): If I stop by your place I'll have to make a detour, I'm very busy, I mean I don't have much time, I need to go here, here, and there. And I have some errands to run beforehand, I mean…

Isabelle (disconcerted): Oh, okay. Yes, maybe…

Peter (revising): Well what I want to say or to be clearer at least…

Isabelle (not letting him finish): It's just that, you understand, my bag is really heavy so I thought that maybe…

Peter: I know someone who always carry heavy bag, to be more precise…

Peter bursts out laughing. He suddenly realizes the situation and concludes, "I'm comfortable helping you, that's OK" What he means here is that each of the two protagonists were needing the perception and channel of communication of their base.

After this exchange, both people realize the situation and match their communication styles. Drivers are not only recognized by words and expressions. Facial expressions can also provide precious information when the person is in front of us. The mere fact of knowing the distress signals helps put a situation into perspective, like this business manager told us.

"I noticed something I find interesting. The fact of understanding the other person helps keep me from being affected by their distress. The Process Communication Model works like a filter that keeps us from feeling hurt and wanting to "get back" at others. It calms many situations. I used to work with a guy who had a Persister base. I have a Persister base. Without this analysis tool, we probably would have had a terrible time communicating. After twenty years on the job, he had forged a great number of certainties. And even though I was younger, I had quite a few of my own! The issue was this: "Do we each keep to ourselves or do we go at each other?" In fact, we kept most of our convictions and I think we enriched one another. We would not have been able to do it if we didn't speak this common language. Another example: my assistant is a wonderful person with a Rebel base. Think about it, a Persister type with a Rebel type! Yet, everything is fine. I think that Process Communication Model helps each person get the best from the other on the job. When the atmosphere "sours" with my assistant, I sometimes tell her, "Oh all right, I just met the Rebel. Can I see her in Thinker now please?" That's when we both laugh. It is an excellent "safety valve" that helps us be efficient again."

Type	Driver	Body language	Behavior	What to do
Harmonizer	Please you	Raised eyebrows. Shoulders in. Head Nodding with chin tucked.	Words: "maybe, a little, you know, kinda". Plaintive tone of voice that rises at the end of the sentence. Over adapts.	Use Emotions and the nurturative channel to show warmth, understanding and goodwill.
Thinker	Be Perfect for you	Punctuating with fingers or the hand. Robot like posture. Pressured facial expression.	Unneeded qualifications in statements. Over-details, does not delegate well. Over thinks for others. Staccato tone of voice.	Use Thoughts and the Requestive channel while recognizing the other's knowledge and competence.
Rebel	Try Hard for you	Struggling, wrinkled facial expressions. Palms up with wrists cocked. Leaning forward, bent down, head up, shrugged shoulders.	"I can't", "I don't know", "um, huh". Not answering a direct question. Strained, pressured tone of voice. Inappropriately delegates so that others will be responsible.	Use Reactions and the Emotive channel, joke, chat or take a break.

Imaginer	Be Strong for you	Molded, blank, expressionless. No gestures, if only a finger on the chin.	Monotonic tone of voice. Words: "It just occurred to me, sometimes I, that makes me feel." Believes that things or people are in charge of their emotions or thoughts.	Use Reflections and the Directive channel aiming at behavior. Examples: "Present the report to me", "Make me a summary".
Persister	Be Perfect for me	Calculated gestures. Rigid, aloof posture. Head cocked up, severe.	Over questioning, big words when little would do. Asks complicated question. Precise tone of voice. Focuses on what is wrong rather than what's right.	Use Opinions and the Requestive channel while recognizing the person's high standards and call attention to positive points.
Promoter	Be Strong for me	Robot-like gestures. Stone-like postures. Stone-faced, hard facial expressions. Few eye blinks.	"What made you think..?", "How did he make you feel?". Uses "you" when meaning "I" in referring to self. Monotonous tone of voice. Expects others to fend for themselves.	Use Actions and the Directive channel with challenges and risks.

SECOND DEGREE MISCOMMUNICATION: MASKS AND FAILURE MECHANISMS

If we are in first degree distress of our phase, there is a risk that we will fall into second degree distress of the phase. While the first degree is not easily perceived, the second one "jumps out" at us. The tone of voice changes, as well as the facial expressions. Emotional expression is very clear, though it does not exist in the first degree. The person wears an easily identifiable second degree mask that depends on their personality type: Attacker mask for the Persister and Thinker types, Blamer mask for the Rebel and Promoter types, and Drooper for the Harmonizer and Imaginer types.

In second degree distress, the content of the exchange appears to be the most important when in reality the protagonists are unconsciously trying to satisfy a psychological need. Someone who wears a second degree mask is simply someone who is "hungry".

During a "serious" meeting, Isabelle feels, "No one pays attention to me here." She intervenes timidly, "I know I'm going to say something stupid…" Which tends to bring on an irritated reply like, "All right, all right, we don't have time to waste on that."

A person will activate their failure mechanism when in second degree distress. This is unconscious behavior aimed at satisfying the psychological need, only negatively. Failure mechanisms have harmful effects on business and/or family life and friendships. For example, by making stupid mistakes, she could be rejected; by imposing his convictions, he could cause conflict and/or disinterest from others; by passively waiting, she could end up entirely isolated and no one will speak to her, etc.

For each personality type, we find the same characteristics under "normal" pressure only exaggerated:

- The Thinker type who functions based on thought, will attack on thoughts, intelligence and competence.
- The Persister type will attack on the basis of their opinions and and topics like morals and commitment, etc.
- The Harmonizer type will do anything to be negatively recognized as a person.
- The Rebel type will escalate the conflict to obtain their dose of contact.
- The Promoter type will find excitement in manipulation.
- The Imaginer type will disconnect the circuits linking them to the outside world.

Attacker Mask

It is worn by people with Persister and Thinker bases or phases.

Figure 6.2: Attacker Mask

Thinker Type: "Here comes the cop"

In second degree distress, the Thinker type will become irritated because others are not intelligent, competent or don't understand. This type attacks within the intellectual sphere and/or their favorite themes of money and tidiness: "Clean this mess up!", "The kids toys don't belong on the living room floor, they belong in their room!", "Have you ever heard of something called a budget?", "You are stupid!"

Jack gets home late one evening. It had been a rough day. He wasn't satisfied with the quality of the report he had just given his boss, Peter. Peter, who had been very preoccupied as well, barely glanced at it before adding it to the pile of urgent business. Jack held it in all day but when he got home, it was too much: coats and boots were strewn all over the entryway and dinner wasn't ready. "It was too much for me," he would say later, "I was really angry and everyone got a taste of it."

People with a Thinker phase often show excellent self-control at the office and 'let off steam' when they get home. "We're a lot calmer when you're at work, Dad", or "Whenever you come home, it's to rank and scream", hears the Dad who arrives home late. This adds another dose of stress to an already hellish day. At the second degree of miscommunication we can observe the failure mechanism which for the Thinker type is over-controlling. "Here comes the cop," teased the wife of a senior executive when he got home from the office in a huff. When in distress, the Thinker type manager will tend to think, "I can do it better and faster than everyone else", "It's true that I work a lot; I don't have anyone competent around."

The first impact of over-control on managers is causing loss of motivation. "Why bother finishing since he's going to do it all over anyway." In second degree distress, people with a Thinker type reinforce over-controlling to the extent of isolating themselves and having to juggle twice the workload.

Thinker Type Failure Mechanism: Over-Controlling

Persister Type: "They haven't heard the end of me"

The Persister type wears an Attacker mask. This type will tend to become rigid, suspicious, and stop listening. The person attacks on matters of opinion and can throw some infamous "tantrums". While the Thinker type tends to express cold anger, the Persister type explodes like a pressure-cooker. The other person, "isn't responsible on their job", "is unaware", "has no ethics", "has the morals of an alley cat", etc.

This type's failure mechanism is to crusade: storms a Persister type manager to his Rebel type employee in an attempt to make an impression. "What entitles you to speak to me like that? Are you aware of the terrible example you are setting for young people? You should start by taking a hard look at yourself".

The tone of voice is overbearing. Sentences contain definitive statements. The person does not listen, interrupts, finishes others' sentences for them. While this type's need is to "convey" their opinions, they instead encourage coworkers, employees or their children to "wait out the storm" or react in conflictual escalation.

Another characteristic of the Persister type in second degree distress: this type becomes very sensitive to negative feedback even when appropriate. If we need to point out a weak spot to a person with a Persister phase, it is recommended to carefully manage the process because the person could react strongly and take the feedback as criticism.

Persister Type Failure Mechanism: Crusading

Blamer Mask

This mask is worn by the Rebel and Promoter types.

Figure 6.3: Blamer Mask

Rebel Type: "It's not my fault, I..."

"What? What about my report?!" answers the Rebel type employee in a provocative tone, "It's not my fault it's not finished yet." This is followed by a long description intended to put the blame on others. This type's unconscious goal is to satisfy their need for contact. A favorite phrase is, "It's not my fault". The person will deploy their creative talent to the extent of bad faith, finding an entire range of great – and irritating – reasons to demonstrate: "it isn't my fault".

In second degree distress, the Rebel type often shows a lot of finesse in detecting the other person's weak spot and subtly pushing that button just to see how the other person will react. In other words, 'The art of making someone feel guilty'. Another characteristic of the Rebel type wearing a Blamer mask: they sometimes play "Yes, but"[14].

- I don't know what to do.
- Maybe you could try this.
- Yes, I tried but...
- On the other hand, if you did that.
- Yes, but...

Until the moment when the person concludes that, "Anyway, I knew I wouldn't be able to come up with a good idea."

By blaming – this type's failure mechanism – the Rebel type has every chance to begin a resounding escalation. This quarrel can lead to a break-up. It is as if in those moments, the Rebel type tries to provoke rejection. "If you keep that up you're going to get fired." Answer: "Oh, I know very well that's what you want anyway." Since this profile lives in the moment, distressed Rebel personality types do not measure the consequences of their acts: they are therefore very likely to "escalate" very strongly and very quickly.

It is interesting to note that as soon as they "take a hit", people with a Rebel type feel relieved! As if the fact pleased them. They receive a few barbed remarks and smile broadly, which only further irritates the other person who thinks, "And to top it off, she laughs at me." Well, no. The Rebel type feels pleasure because they obtained their "dose" of contact: "You're angry at me, so you are paying attention to me." Let's remember

---

14   Eric Berne. The Games People Play, op. cit.

that this profile's existential question is: "Am I acceptable?" In other words, "Do you accept me the way I am and the way I do things?" This should not be confused with the existential question for the Harmonizer type, "Am I loveable?" In other words, do you love me for who I am?"

Rebel Type Failure Mechanism: Blaming

Promoter Type: The art of making mischief

The failure mechanism for the Promoter type is manipulation. In second degree distress, people with this type set themselves up for "negative challenges". "I bet I can get him to do my job for me", "I bet I can get him to sign", etc. The aim of this behavior is to obtain negative excitement. Another means is taking dangerous risks for their health, their safety, their business, etc. or else making mischief by creating tension between people. The Promoter type in distress is a great player of "Let's You and Him Fight"[15]. In any case, "something has to happen". In a business context, they can engage in acrobatics with unpredictable consequences on the market or client. In a private context, this type can also find excitement in conducting several romances at the same time. Another tendency of the Promoter type in distress: to mock and use sarcasm, which they confuse with humor. "Where'd you get your degree? No way, I'm hallucinating! They give it to anybody over there!" Imagine the reaction of the employee with a Thinker type who is singled out this way by a Promoter type boss.

Promoter Type Failure Mechanism: Manipulating

Drooper Mask

When in second degree distress, the Harmonizer and Imaginer types wear a Drooper mask.

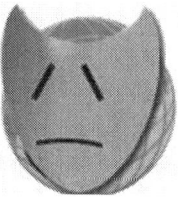

Figure 6.3: Drooper Mask

---

[15]   Eric Berne, op. cit.

Harmonizer Type: "It always happens to me"

The Drooper Mask: can be characterized by complaining, playing victim, and saying "nobody loves me". This attitude tends to cause two types of reactions: flight ("Get me outta here!") or attack ("Here, I'll give you something to cry about").

After trying to "please" and be loved, the Harmonizer type in distress will stop thinking clearly and start interpreting any negative information as, "I don't love you". The person's quest for recognition can be totally misunderstood or seem inappropriate. The person does not directly ask for what they really need but deploys a whole series of strategies to obtain their "dose" of recognition.

The Harmonizer-Thinker couple can lead to dialogues like this: "Do you love me?" Vaguely annoyed, the Thinker type answers: "Listen, why should I waste my time telling you I love you? It's obvious. All you need to know is that the day it's no longer the case, I'll let you know".

The failure mechanism for the Harmonizer type consists in making stupid involuntary mistakes that will get them negative recognition. In second degree distress, the Harmonizer type person feels sad and depressed; it's all going wrong and it's all their fault.

Harmonizer Type Failure Mechanism: Making Mistakes

Imaginer Type: "Quiet on the set"

On the other hand, the Imaginer type takes a more discreet victim position. In first degree distress, they tend to withdraw. In second degree, the failure mechanism will be passive waiting: they stop doing anything. A person with this type profile will totally withdraw, both psychologically and/or physically (sick leave, for example). They lose their ability to concentrate and disperse themselves across several tasks with the feeling that they will never have the time.

While the Harmonizer mask does not go unnoticed, the Imaginer type mask grows in silence. Their facial expressions are impassive and they deliver even less personal information than usual. Sometimes, loved ones misunderstand this distress. The person does not seem to be feeling particularly well but it's all so discreet.

Imaginer Type Failure Mechanism: Waiting Passively

Figure 6.2: Masks and Failure Mechanisms by Personality Type

Mask	Personality type	Failure mechanism
Drooper 	Harmonizer	Makes mistakes
Drooper 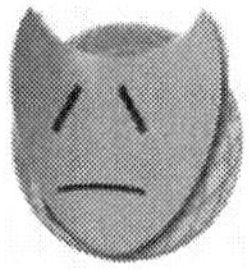	Imaginer	Waits passively
Attacker 	Thinker	Over-controls
Attacker 	Persister	Crusades
Blamer 	Rebel	Blames
Blamer 	Promoter	Manipulates

MANAGING SECOND DEGREE MASKS

As we have seen, first degree masks consist in subtle behavior that is often hard to detect. However, second degree masks are accompanied by a more or less intense emotional charge and are easy to identify. If we want to reestablish communication, we must meet the psychological needs expressed through failure mechanisms.

Table 6.3: Failure Mechanisms and Intervention Strategies

You see	You know	You can
Someone who criticizes everything you say or do, who has trouble delegating, considers others as incompetent and over-controls.	That this is the behavior of the Thinker type in distress who is wearing an Attacker mask.	recognizing their competence.
Someone climbing on their high horse, who becomes brittle, interrupts others without listening and crusades.	That this is the behavior of the Persister type in distress who is wearing an Attacker mask.	listening to their opinions and respecting them even if you don't agree with them.
Someone who shifts the blame, who complains, is bored, doesn't know what to do and blames others.	That this is the behavior of the Rebel type in distress who is wearing a Blamer mask.	Be playful with the person.
Someone who is driven, who only seeks extreme sensations, who manipulates or creates tension between others, spreads rumors.	That this is the behavior of the Promoter type in distress who is wearing a Blamer mask.	responding to the need for excitement with challenges or by creating highly stimulating situations.
Someone who seems to be losing their footing, becoming clingy or whiny, feels victimized, burdened, who carries the weight of the world on their shoulders and who makes mistakes.	That this is the behavior of the Harmonizer type in distress who is wearing a Drooper mask.	Recognize the person for who they are
Someone who is "not there", eyes on the horizon and who waits passively.	That this is the behavior of the Imaginer type in distress who is wearing a Drooper mask.	Encourage the person to spend time by themselves

Summary

There are three second degree masks:

- Attacker: for the Thinker and Persister types
- Blamer: for the Rebel and Promoter types
- Drooper: for the Harmonizer and Imaginer types.

This is the level of miscommunication on which people will display their failure mechanism in the aim of obtaining negative satisfaction of their psychological needs since they are unable to satisfy them positively. The failure mechanisms are:

- Over-controlling for the Thinker type
- Crusading for the Persister type
- Blaming for the Rebel type
- Manipulating for the Promoter type
- Making mistakes for the Harmonizer type
- Waiting passively for the Imaginer type.

THIRD DEGREE MISCOMMUNICATION

The third degree of miscommunication corresponds to a state of severe, sustained distress. The corresponding mask is the Despairer mask. An individual in third degree distress has not obtained satisfaction of their physical, emotional, or spiritual needs for a long period of time and even the negative benefits they are able to derive from second degree distress are not satisfying. The person's position is one of, "I'm not OK, You're not OK either". They feel trapped, confined. This kind of behavior is not often encountered in the workplace because people in this position often leave their jobs for a while and require appropriate care. All of the failure mechanisms can lead to this same point: the loss of hope and its corollary, depression. This is the level on which the person "reaps" the negative end-benefits of what is presented below. All personality types can reach the third degree and wear a Despairer mask. However, their inner experience will vary from the solitary Imaginer type's "Why bother?" to the aggressive Promoter type's "I've nothing left to lose".

Table 6.4: Third Degree Mask and Negative End-Benefit

Personality type	Negative end-benefit
Thinker	Is rejected or rejects others: "They're stupid"
Persister	Is rejected or rejects others: "They don't believe in me"
Rebel	Is rejected and vengeful: "They'll just wait and see"
Promoter	Is rejected or rejects others, mocks them: "Poor jerk, you've got no guts"
Harmonizer	Is rejected: "I knew they didn't love me"
Imaginer	Is rejected: "No one told me what I was supposed to do"

LIFE POSITIONS AND DRAMA TRIANGLE

Life Positions

Life positions were identified by Eric Berne[16]. According to him, the +/+ position is the healthy position for the best quality of life. This is the one we access within the first months of life, or else later on at the price of hard work. It cannot be achieved by mere desire. Our life position, he adds, depends on our belief in ourselves, in others, and in life.

In PCM, +/+ position is the only existential life position. All other life positions are behavioral.

When we are not in the +/+ position, we are in miscommunication. There are 4 combinations:

Me	You
+ I'm OK	+ You're OK
+ I'm OK	- You're not OK
- I'm not OK	+ You're OK
- I'm not OK	- You're not OK

Our life position at a given moment will determine our "interpretation" of the world. For example:

---

16   Eric Berne. *What Do You Say After You Say Hello?*

Stimulus: I see someone look at me and smile.

+/+: I see kindness and I smile back in response; I'm unsure of the meaning of the smile; I question the person verbally or non-verbally.

+/-: I think the person already looks silly, and when they smile…

-/+: What's wrong with me? Why is he making fun of me?

-/-: You really have to be bad off to smile at someone like me.

Stimulus: Meeting with a prospect who is showing impatience.

+/+: This man probably has a Thinker phase and is distressed. I will reassure him that we will be brief and that we will get right down to the essentials.

+/-: This guy isn't even able to control himself.

-/+: I'll never be able to do it. He's going to throw me out.

-/-: (in despair) With a guy like that I'm going to screw up again.

Stimulus: I meet with a "go-getter" client.

+/+: How to invite him into a win-win position?

+/-: This is going to be bloody. He'll see.

-/+: This guy intimidates me. I'm sure I'm going to get ripped off.

-/-: I'm an idiot to be doing a job like this with people like him.

Unlike the other life positions, in +/+ we try to seek information before interpreting the meaning of another person's behavior. The +/+ relationship is by far the most efficient. However, since it is not "natural", it requires vigilance on our part and that we invest energy to maintain it. Throughout the day we can alternate between the four positions depending on the circumstances, who the other person is, and our level of distress.

MANAGING MISCOMMUNICATION

We have seen the right strategies for breaking out of miscommunication in its first and second degrees. Applying this strategy requires that we have a high level of energy to enable us to take the elevator and use the appropriate floor.

What do we do when we feel "stuck" in distress, with little energy to manage the process? It is important not to "force" ourselves by trying to play on the Harmonizer, Thinker, Rebel register, etc. It is essential to remain ourselves. This is the very basis of all communication.

One effective technique is to listen to what is happening. The person realizes they are "stuck" by the other person's behavior and are in distress. We remember that our elevator gets blocked when we are in distress so we can no longer reach the right floor to manage the process. Awareness of our level of distress helps us take a step back and gain perspective. For instance, saying to the other person, "I'm going to take some time to think about what's going on. We'll continue later. Does that suit you?" helps avoid the risk of getting bogged down in miscommunication.

Concerning life positions, we have seen that the +/+ position requires an investment in energy to maintain it. As soon as we are in distress we all find our "preferred" life position (usually +/- or -/+) in which, as we recall, we perceive the other as not being as OK as we or vice versa, we see ourselves as inferior to the other (-/+). In this case, we don't always want to use the right channel. It is not always easy to say, "I love you" to someone with a very strong Please driver. With a very strong Try Hard driver, it is easier to answer, "You annoy me" than "Let's laugh a little". With a super Be Perfect driver, we feel more like interrupting the sermon with, "You bore me".

Meta-communicating means making an offer like, "Can we talk about what's going on between us?" If the other person answers, "Okay, let's talk about it", it is the signal that they have returned to their thinking part and that it is possible to exchange information. The problem can then be worded like, "What is difficult for me right now is that you gave me a lot of information and I have trouble keeping up." Or, "I realize that you have high expectations of me and I am not available to answer right now". Or, "I feel it would be good for us to start with a little fun, don't you think?" By verifying through the initial offer that they can meta-communicate, people give themselves every chance of resolving communication problems. Plus, this kind of exercise strengthens the relationship since each person feels considered in terms of their needs. **We haven't found anything better for understanding one another than talking to each other.**

Sylvia, with a Harmonizer base in Rebel phase, is in distress. "This job is so long and complicated." She feels as if she will never get through it. She feels it just isn't getting anywhere. From within her, the cry of the Harmonizer type in second degree distress rises in her throat, "Help! I'm cracking up!" She can only show powerlessness to her superior,

"Gosh, it's just not moving. I'm so discouraged". As bad luck would have it, Thomas has all of the characteristics of a person in Promoter phase. His face freezes, he says nothing for several seconds then says coldly, "Didn't you assure me the job would be done by the end of the week?" meaning, "I will be very disappointed if it isn't done". What Sylvia hears is "If you're not capable, that's your problem." Plus, Thomas attacks her all the time, which is her weak spot. She makes super-human efforts to answer him and defend her position but her voice trails off, her arguments are unconvincing, and she feels torn between panic and anger. Meanwhile, her manager unconsciously tries to satisfy his need: getting the job done is exciting and should be done quickly to be able to enjoy the personal and professional benefits from it: fame and fortune.

Neither of the two protagonists have enough energy to give the other their preferred psychological needs and manage the process. They are both in distress. However, one of them can offer to meta-communicate. In order to restore the relationship, Thomas could say for example, "Our relationship is important to me. You're important to me. I propose that we take a minute to think about this problem. Does you feel OK?" Sylvia's energy level instantly rises. "I'd love to", she answers. Her expression is sharper, her complexion is clearer, she sits up straight in her chair. Thomas feels definite pleasure in observing this change in attitude.

In a few instants, once they listen to each other, each person expresses their inner experience, their mixed fear and anger and they find themselves talking to someone who is attentive and understanding. Soon the job does not seem as long or complicated to Sylvia, especially since it has already come along. Thomas realizes that he put pressure on her for no purpose and did not support her enough when she ran into difficulties. "What do you need to finish this job?" he asks. In a few words, a "revved up" Sylvia makes two or three proposals that Thomas accepts, telling her what a precious employee she is.

CHAPTER 7

FAILURE PATTERNS

Eric Berne identified six "scripts" or negative "blueprints for life" that appeared to serve as patterns of behavior that a person repeats over the course of life, over varying timeframes. Transactional Analysis theorists most commonly thought that these scripts developed from "script injunctions" or negative messages that were received by the person over the course of his or her life. Taibi Kahler conducted research into the formation and nature of scripts over course of his career and discovered that scripts were created and reinforced by Drivers and that a person's particular script was determined by his or her Personality Structure. Injunctions play no role in their formation. He discovered that, prior to experiencing a Phase change, a person's script was the one associated with his or her Base Personality Type, that, following a Phase Change, depending on the Personality Type associated with the Phase Type, the script could change and that certain scripts were associated with unique combinations of Base and Phase. Over time, in order to differentiate his conclusions from those of the other TA theorists, he stopped referring to them as "scripts" and renamed them "failure patterns."

SIX FAILURE PATTERNS

The research Taibi Kahler conducted enables us to associate one of the six failure patterns to each Personality Type. When someone suffers a setback in business or their private lives it is often due to one of these failure patterns: Until, After, Never, Always, Almost I, Almost II.

Until

People with an "Until" failure pattern behave as though they think, "I can't enjoy it as long as I haven't", "I can't have fun before", and they put satisfaction off for later. "When I have the time, I'll go see the Matisse exhibit.", "I can't take any time off until I've finished my job.", "I'll see this battle through to the end, no matter what the cost."

Their driver is Be Perfect for you or Be Perfect for me. Their personality types are Thinker and Persister. In business life they can think things like, "I know it's late. I know the kids are waiting for me, that I'm tired and not very efficient at this hour. But I can't go home until this presentation is entirely finished." or, "I know I need to take a break to renew my energy and be functional again. But I just can't pull myself away from my desk." Or, as they leave a training seminar, "It was very good but I can't use that model until I've perfectly mastered it."

In their personal lives, people with an Until failure pattern can "drain the cup of bitterness": "My marriage is a failure but I committed myself. I'll see it through."

In everyday life, these people also set themselves restrictions like, "I can't go to bed before the dishes are done", "I can't relax until the house is clean", "I won't go on vacation as long as I haven't finished the home improvement jobs."

Connection Between Driver and Failure Pattern

As we saw above[17] Thinker and Persister types under the influence of the Be Perfect driver can go so far as to sacrifice their private lives. They need to work first and have fun later, if there's enough time. If they are not careful, they allow their jobs to progressively nibble away at their free time and will no longer be available for spouse and children.

> "Every Sunday afternoon, I force myself to take a walk with my wife," says a person with a Thinker base. I feel like this walk is an obligation because I could be doing more useful things with my time. In fact, my wife is always frustrated at the end of our walk because she says I don't talk enough and that I seem tense and preoccupied."

---

[17] See negative satisfaction of psychological needs, Chapter 3

Some Characteristics of the Until Failure Pattern

Unable to stop working; does not put time limits on work. Goes "all the way", at whatever the cost. Is irritated when interrupted or "bothered". Unavailable to others. Only realizes his mistakes once he experiences them. Shows real determination to finish what he starts.

After

People with an "After" failure pattern tend to behave as though "Everything's fine for now, but sooner or later, something bad is going to happen." "This is going to end badly." "It's too good to be true." There must be problems on the horizon. They feel anxiety and are afraid that things are too good to last.

Their driver is Please you; their personality type Harmonizer.

They often build their sentences in two parts separated by an implicit or explicit conditional "but". "I feel good but with the meal we're having tonight I'll probably have problems. I love this kind of party but I never remember what anyone says."

In private life, the After failure pattern leads to definitive conclusions like, "He's a great guy but I just can't believe he's interested in me. I know it won't last." "I'm fine for now but I'm afraid I'll get sick and die." "The kids are having fun at camp but I'm afraid something will happen to them."

In business life: "I've done everything to please but the others are still angry with me." "I reached my objectives but I got lucky. I'm afraid I won't make it next time." "Things are running smoothly for now but do you think it's going to last?"

Connection Between Driver and Failure Pattern

A person with a Harmonizer personality type who tries to please will tend to say yes to everyone, to "sacrifice" him or herself for others. For instance, they make promises to everyone but fail to keep their commitments.

Some Characteristics of the After Failure Pattern

Expects disaster. Tends to be pessimistic, anxious, and discouraged. Fear of the future. Inhibition towards initiative.

Never

People with a "Never" failure pattern behave as though they think, "I can never seem to get what I want." "I spread myself too thin." "I'll never make it." The driver is Be Strong; personality type Imaginer.

They tend to start things without finishing them. When they do not end communication, they express themselves by jumping from one subject to another. "I used to... then ... oh, I don't know if you remember... Peter was saying that..."

In private life, the person with a Never failure pattern would say, for example, "I can never make any friends." "I would like to get married and have a family but I can never meet the right person." In business life, "I don't have time. I'm too slow." "No one would ever consider me for a promotion."

Connection Between Driver and Failure Pattern

The Imaginer type in first degree distress shows a Be Strong for you driver. They withdraw, become too passive and are unable to obtain what they seek. Example:

Anne made a lot of friends during a group trip. At the end, everyone promised to get together again. And in fact, two or three times, Anne was invited to these get-togethers. But, since she preferred to be alone, she always refused the invitation. No one has called in over six months. Anne still suffers from not having any friends.

Some Characteristics of the After Failure Pattern

Frequent dissatisfaction. Life in a "dotted line": unable to draw a full line, there are always breaks in it. Can give a feeling of vagueness and confusion. Hesitation. Apathy. Passive hyper-lucidity: perceives things very well but does nothing.

Always

People with an "Always" failure pattern behave as though they think, "It won't work. Whatever I do, I'm stuck." "If I go down now to put money in the meter, I'll miss the best part of the movie. If I don't go now, I'll get a ticket for sure."

Their driver is Try Hard and Be Strong for me; personality types Rebel and Promoter.

In private life, a young man with a Rebel base could say, "If I go to Greece on vacation, I'll relax but I won't see my best buddies for a month. If I stay, I won't really take advantage of my vacation or my freedom. I don't know what to do. I'm stuck." Result: impossible to decide until all the flights are full! Other options: "I have two invitations for Saturday night. I can't decide." "I would like to get married but I don't want to lose my freedom."

> A sales manager with a Promoter base buys superb clothes with his credit card. He justifies this with, "I have to buy great clothes because if I didn't I couldn't show myself to my clients. But my commission didn't come in this month. I'm stuck. If I buy myself these clothes they'll cancel my card on me. If I don't buy them, I won't be able to do business. Whatever I do, I'm stuck." He does not consider any other options for resolving the problem.

In business life: "If I accept his promotion, I'll have to move, but I don't want to leave this house, but if I refuse, I'll stagnate." Another example: "If I give this assignment to Peter, Paul will be frustrated, but if I give it to Paul, Peter will be frustrated."

Connection Between Driver and Failure Pattern

Tom, with a Be Strong for me driver can't stand people who are dependent. Single life no longer excites him. He wants to make a "super marriage". The problem is that as soon as he seduces the woman he dreams of marrying, he loses interest and doesn't want to pursue the relationship. He is afraid of having a "wife to support" and moves on to a new conquest. "I've had enough of single life but I just can't decide. I'm stuck."

Some Characteristics of the Always Failure Pattern

"All or nothing", wanting everything that leads nowhere. Whims. Indecision or else determined, barges ahead, regrets his choices. Does not know how to renounce. Can seem constantly frustrated or optimistic.

The roadmaps need revision: there are plenty of roads but none of them are the right one.

Almost I

People with an "Almost I" failure pattern are almost successful, but not quite. "Oh, if only…" Their driver is Try Hard and Please you; their personality type is Harmonizer in Rebel phase or Rebel in Harmonizer phase.

If you give them a job for the 20th, it is possible that it won't be finished until the 21st. If they decide to run 5K, they will often stop at 4. Or they will decide to take a training course and stop before the final exam, etc. They are always ready to stop before having entirely finished. There is always a "grain of sand" that keeps the project from completion. A grain of sand that they unconsciously place there themselves.

In private life, it leads to stories like, "I decided to go on a diet and lose 10 pounds. I lost 8, everything was fine. And then there was a megafeast at some friends' and wham! I'm back to square one." Or "I forgot to pay my taxes and I got a 10% penalty." or "I was tired of having money problems so I drew up a really good budget. I noted my spending every night. I was almost out of the red. But then, I got a chance for a fantastic getaway with some friends and boom!"

In business life, this failure pattern could, for instance, cause them to quarrel with a client two minutes before signing a carefully prepared contract, or hand in an excellent report but with no conclusion, or they forget the slides that they had so carefully prepared for the meeting at home.

Phrases from people with an Almost I failure pattern often build a series of positive points concluded by one negative point that cancels out all the others. "It's really great here. We're really comfortable, the boss is nice, we can use the ping-pong tables and pool as much as we want, the countryside is gorgeous but the clientele sucks."

Some Characteristics of the Almost I Failure Pattern

Coming in fourth in the Olympics. Incompletion. The busy bee who works hard but never manages to finish. People sometimes call them "unlucky". The person who fails on the last yard line, misses their train, plane, runs out of gas.

Almost II

People with an "Almost II" failure pattern feel a sensation of emptiness, even collapse after completing a project. "Now that I've made it, what do I do now? Is that all there is?"

This feeling can cause them to quit their job for no apparent reason. In private life, they feel they have obtained what they want (the Almost II failure pattern is one of social success) but strangely, it hasn't made them any happier.

Their drivers are Please and Be Perfect for you or Be Perfect for me; their personality type Thinker or Persister in Harmonizer phase or Harmonizer in Thinker or Persister phase.

Example of an Almost II failure pattern in private life, "I have everything to be happy, yet..." "I dreamed so much of having this car and now that I'm behind the wheel, I don't feel anything at all."

In business life, at the end of the year, the boss tells his staff, "This year we reached our objectives but let's not be mistaken, we benefited from an excellent economy which won't happen again soon." (Response from a Thinker Rebel type: "Oh, really? It was the economy? And what about us in all that?").

If they are not attentive to their needs, people in an Almost II failure pattern can feel depressed or even collapse when a job is completed and can easily find themselves in situations with no intimate contact or joy.

Some Characteristics of the Almost II Failure Pattern

The "fear of success" syndrome. The person revises everything. Their weakness: always more, always higher. Do not know how to enjoy what they have. Have forgotten the feeling of joy in being alive.

FAILURE PATTERN INTENSITY

When in distress, each person can experience their failure pattern to varying degrees of intensity.

Table 7.1: A Failure Pattern with Varying Degrees of Intensity

Failure pattern	"Hard" version	"Soft" version
Until	The workaholic who gets divorced because he never prioritized his marriage. A manager who dies of heart attack when he retires.	A manager who feels uncomfortable leaving his office because he hasn't finished the job he wanted to get done.
After	A mother who overprotects her child for fear of something happening to it, who feels anxious when the child is out of her sight.	A manager who worries that something might go wrong with the project.
Never	"My life is a failure."	"I never could learn how to swim."
Always	Ending up in prison.	Hesitating, having trouble deciding.
Almost I	Getting fired for always being late.	Promising themselves to wish a happy birthday, then forgetting the date and calling the day after.
Almost II	Reaching the "promised land" and suffering a breakdown.	Refusing a compliment or thanks with, "It's nothing; it's only normal."

Awareness of our failure pattern behavior helps free up energy for a happier life, makes us more efficient in managing our lives and enables more satisfying relationships with others. It also helps us more easily identify this behavior in others and act accordingly. As an illustration, table 7.2 lists this behavior in business life and the appropriate response from the manager.

Table 7.2: Some Possible Responses to Failure Pattern Behavior

Failure pattern	Signs	Manager response
Until	The Thinker or Persister type employee cannot pull himself away from his files, splits hairs, over-controls. Cannot take a step back until the file is *perfectly* completed.	Provide information on needs satisfaction, encourage reading or stress management or time management training courses. Recognize performance
After	The Harmonizer type employee who tries to please everyone, does not know how to say no and causes situations of frustration and rejection.	Encourage the employee to affirm herself, to set limits and suggest the goal of becoming aware of her limits and learning to say no. Recognize person
Never	The Imaginer type employee does not have time to finish his task, he gives up and starts another, has the impression of never being able to finish.	Encourage the employee to finish one task before going on to another while respecting the person's need for quiet.
Always	The Rebel or Promoter type employee feels "stuck", is unable to prioritize; becomes intolerant to frustration.	Provide contact/ incidence
Almost I	The employee tends to fail just before completion.	Support the employee in the final stages.
Almost II	The employee feels depressed or with low energy after having achieved a goal.	Suggest celebrating the success.

CHAPTER 8

PERSONALITY INVENTORY

Knowing the Personality Types helps us to identify our key behaviors and those of others. Although the skills taught in PCM will give us the ability through mere observation in determining a persons base and phase sometimes a more in depth and complete Personality Structure will be necessary. The Personality Pattern Inventory, or PPI, a questionnaire developed by Taibi Kahler that measures the order and strength of each floor of a person's Condominium to include Phases and Stages.

PERSONALITY INVENTORY STRUCTURE

When a person takes the PPI, the result is a computer generated profile report that shows:

- The Personality Structure;
- The energy level available at each floor of their Condominium;
- The current Phase;
- Predictable reactions in distress, both Phase distress and, for those who have Phased, Base distress;
- Their preferred Communication Channels.

Your PPI profile report informs us on the range of interactions, in other words, the person's ability to efficiently communicate with the other Personality Types depending on the available energy level on each floor (the range indicates the proportion of time during which the person will be able to dialogue with the corresponding personality), failure behaviors, management style, etc.

Using the PPI as a recruitment tool is increasingly popular. It enables us to predict which environment will facilitate the expression of a personality and someone's efficiency. It also enables us to form teams based on the range of interactions of each member.

In personal terms, it facilitates awareness of our strong points and potentials, and tells us how to satisfy our own Psychological Needs. It provides precise indications for managing stress.

PERSONALITY PROFILE REPORT
John DOE

Base: **Persister**   Coach: **Gérard COLLIGNON**
Phase: **Thinker**

1) Perceptions	Scores
Opinions	100
Thoughts	73
Actions	36
Reactions (Likes & Dislikes)	27
Inactions	22
Emotions	18

5) Channels of Communication	Scores
Requestive	100
Directive	34
Emotive	25
Nurturative	16

2) Character Strengths	Scores
Dedicated, Observant, Conscientious	100
Responsible, Logical, Organised	70
Adaptable, Persuasive, Charming	33
Spontaneous, Creative, Playful	24
Imaginative, Reflective, Calm	19
Compassionate, Sensitive, Warm	15

6) Environmental Preferences	Scores
One-to-One	100
Group-to-Group	35
Alone	21
Group	17

3) Interaction Styles	Scores
Democratic	100
Autocratic	38
Laissez Faire	29
Benevolent	20

7) Psychological Needs	Scores
Recognition of Work, Conviction	100
Time Structure	70
Incidence	33
Contact	24
Solitude	19
Recognition of Person, Sensory	15

4) Personality Parts	Scores
Computer	100
Director	37
Emoter	28
Comforter	19

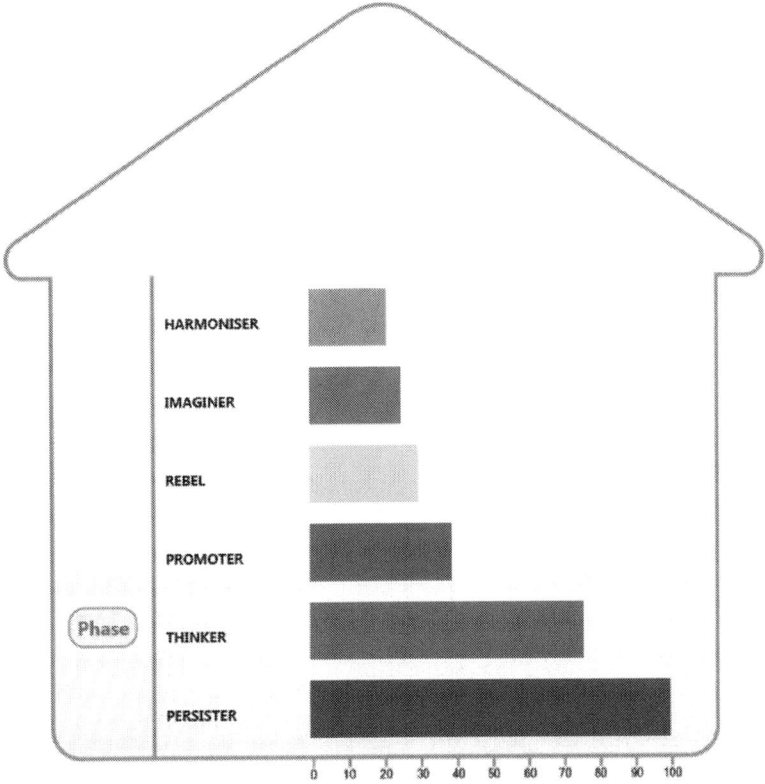

HARMONISER	
IMAGINER	
REBEL	
PROMOTER	
THINKER	
PERSISTER	

0 10 20 30 40 50 60 70 80 90 100

Phase

PHASE DISTRESS SEQUENCE
PHASE: THINKER
Doorway of Distress (1st°)   Be Perfect for you
Basement (2nd°)   Over controls
Cellar (3rd°)   Depressed and worthless

Process Failure Pattern: Until

BASE DISTRESS SEQUENCE
BASE: PERSISTER
Doorway of Distress (1st°)   Be perfect for me
Basement (2nd°)   Pushes Beliefs
Cellar (3rd°)   Depressed and hopeless

Process Failure Pattern: Until

BC: 86, PC: 72

ANALYSIS OF JEREMY DUMONT'S PERSONALITY PROFILE

Jeremy Dumont has a Persister Base and is currently in a Thinker Phase. The secondary characteristics are, in the descending energy order: Promoter, Rebel, Imaginer, and Harmonizer.

Contact Zone: Jeremy Dumont will preferably communicate based on his opinions (he has a score of 100 on this perception). The scores on actions, imagination, reactions and emotions are low. This means he is not very receptive to these Perceptions.

His Characters Strengths are primarily the Characters Strengths of the Persister type, in other words, dedicated, observant, and conscientious. He is currently developing the characteristics of the Thinker type whose Characters Strengths are: responsible, logical, and organized.

Under normal pressure, Jeremy Dumont's *preferred management style* is the Democratic style as a leader and as a follower. He makes relatively little use of the Autocratic, Laissez-faire, and Benevolent styles: scores of 38, 29 and and 20.

Personality Parts: Jeremy Dumont prefers Computer-to-Computer communication based on information exchange. With scores of 37, 28 and 19, the Director, the Emoter and Comforter Personality Parts are rarely used.

Jeremy Dumont prefers to communicate on the Requestive Communication Channel that enables exchange of information. The Directive, the Emotive and Nurturative channels are not often used.

Environmental Preferences: Jeremy Dumont will be most comfortable and work more efficiently in an environment that enables him to work alone or preferably with one other person.

Psychological Needs: this component tells us Jeremy Dumont's current sources of motivation. His Base needs are to be recognized for his work and convictions (Persister type needs). Currently, the most motivating needs will be his phase needs for *Recognition of work and time structure* (Thinker phase needs) in both his business and private life. He desires confirmation that what he has done is noticed. He's motivated by awards, bonuses, a pat on the back – ways of recognizing that they have done a good job. He also needs for knowing what is to be done and when. He needs plan for today, tomorrow, and next week.

Distress Behavior: Several times a day, Jeremy Dumont will show the behavior of the 1° degree of distress of Persister type, demanding perfection from others and will tend to see what is wrong and not what is right.

His Phase Sequence Distress: he will start by using big words, over explaining, over qualifying. He'll also tend to not delegate. He will show the 1° degree of distress of Thinker type.

Then he will show his current *Failure Mechanism:* He will tend to be frustrated with others around thinking issues, to be over-controlling, to be critical of others about fairness, money, order or responsibility.

In the rare event of Base distress, he will tend to try to impose his views, stop listening, analyzing and understanding, and show suspicion or excessive rigor. He will probably tend to become hyper-sensitive to negative feedback even when it is appropriate

The *Failure Pattern*, is the Until Failure Pattern in which the subject can't have fun until he...

Results reliability: BC 86 indicates a high level of reliability for the Base and a normal degree of reliability for the phase (PC 72).

PART 2

Applying The Process Communication Model Concepts

CHAPTER 9

PROCESS COMMUNICATION MODEL:
TAILORED MANAGEMENT

> "*When a person is on the defensive, loss of motivation creeps in, sometimes definitively immobilizing the personal learning process and the probability of change.*" Goleman, Boyatzis, McKee

Many communication problems are due to pressure on the manager. Whether they come from hierarchy or the outside environment, these problems and their damaging consequences could be avoided if the manager had the knowledge and skill to understand the dynamics related to the personality type of each of his or her employees.

Many top managers have a Persister base (about 50% of the clients we meet in our seminars). As we have already seen, the manager with a Persister base is motivated by being heard and getting his message across. This personality type often needs to learn to listen. The ability to listen is the key condition for the appearance of a *new management*[18].

The Process Communication Model is an easily accessible and effective operational tool. Its effectiveness is due to the method's unique adaptability to all levels and types of businesses, people and situations which makes it an excellent way to create a common language. It also addresses one of the essential aspects of business life...understanding what genuinely motivates people.

---

[18]   *L'Entreprise à l'écoute*, 1980.

Despite the model's simplicity, its application requires commitment at the highest level of the organization and real involvement from leadership. The Process Communication Model addresses leadership and provides a series of tools to support them in their learning and experimenting with it: leadership style definition, manager action plans and supervision groups. This chapter is designed as a reference to navigate the path to change.

LEADERSHIP STYLES

> *"Being a good leader requires knowing one's self, identifying one's style and striving to expand it and adjust it."* Meryem Le Saget

Of course, personality types and communication channels intersect with leadership styles. In Process Communication Model we identify four styles, each with its advantages and drawbacks[19].

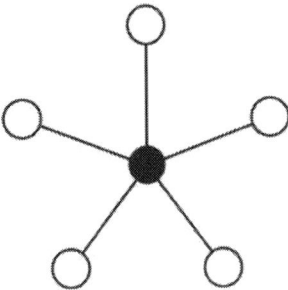

Autocratic Style

The manager gives orders and expects the employees to obey them. He uses the Directive channel and says, for instance, "Make me a summary of this report, please", "Define your objectives for our next meeting, please", "Tell me what...", etc. It is a style that, as we have seen for the Directive channel, addresses the thinking part of the person. It has the advantage of being quick and direct. It helps clearly affirm leadership. Its (sizable) drawback is that it displeases most employees

---

19 The black dot symbolizes the leader and the white dots the employees

whom it invites to rebellion or over-adaptation. It does not encourage feedback. However, it is particularly useful in emergency situations. If there is a fire alarm, we do not consult our staff to decide on the best strategy. We could say it is an "improved military command". Improved because in the army the person is expected to obey. In the Autocratic style they are asked to think in order to obey an order.

It is a style that suits the Imaginer type who needs explicit directives and the Promoter type because it is quick and enables this type to give priority to action. Managers with a Promoter base use it very naturally, which explains why they can encounter leadership problems and can at times be perceived as dictatorial. This style is to be avoided with the other personality types. The employee with a Harmonizer base would think, "Why is he talking to me like that? What have I done?" The Thinker or Persister base employee would think, "I know what I have to do. If he tells me what I have to do it proves he doesn't trust me or thinks I'm incompetent." The employee with a Rebel base will immediately feel "stuck"… and will rebel.

The Autocratic style should therefore be avoided with 85% of the population. However, it is still very widespread and often used in businesses today. An aggravating circumstance is that it sounds very much like a mask. When someone says in a brittle tone, "Do this, period", they are wearing an Attacker mask, which has nothing to do with an Autocratic style based on the +/+ life position. When leaders train in our seminars, they also tend to use this style in an aggressive mode. Use of the positive Autocratic style is often their weak point, which explains the difficulty they sometimes encounter in managing employees with an Imaginer or Promoter base.

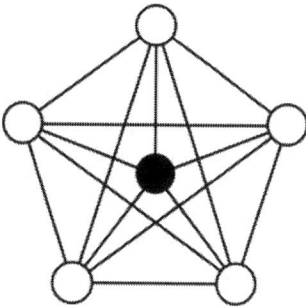

Democratic Style

The leader believes it is fundamental for each person on the team to express their opinions, suggestions and desires. He will make a summary of it on which to base his decision, taking each person's opinion into consideration.

The tremendous advantage of this style is that it mobilizes the company's intelligence. People feel recognized for their analyses, ideas, and suggestions. Its drawback is that it discourages people who need to begin by taking action. It can also be time consuming in the sense that it requires a lot of meetings. One last drawback is that it can create frustrations if the leader is not attentive to the needs for recognition of the Persister type, for example, who strongly defends positions that may not be retained.

However, this style works very well with people who have a Persister or Thinker Base. It should be avoided with employees who have a Promoter base because they will lack stimulation and could show impatience during meetings, drumming their fingers on the table thinking, "What is all this blah blah blah? When do we get to the action?"

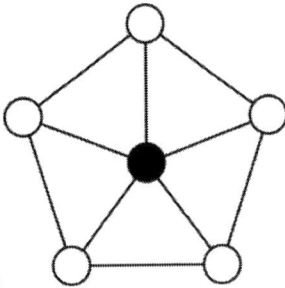

Benevolent Style

The leader is convinced that it is important to have a close, tightly knit team where the atmosphere is pleasant. His ideal team is similar to a family: the company "runs" because it is a bit like a big family where everyone feels at home.

This leadership style is ideal for people who need to be considered as individuals. But most employees, particularly those with a Persister or Thinker base are uncomfortable with it. They often see it as a form of paternalism (which is not a Harmonizer style; it is found more among the Persister type managers of another era), or as an intrusion into their private lives. This is especially true since the leader with a Harmonizer type does not always establish a clear boundary between private time and business time, often encouraging get-togethers on weekends that include spouses and children.

However, this style is remarkably effective with the 30% of the population with a Harmonizer base.

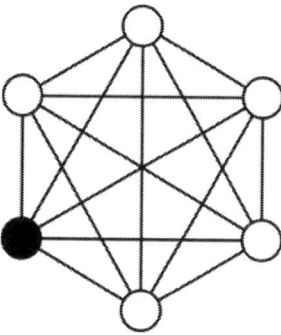

Laissez-faire style

The leader proposes letting each person enjoy as much autonomy as possible. The great advantage of this style is that it fosters creativity and is particularly appropriate for brainstorming. It also works well when each employee has already developed their own personal style of efficiency. Its major drawback is that, for many employees, this style lacks structure. It can cause serious loss of energy when each person is on their own and does a little of everything and anything at the same time. It is particularly suitable with the creative Rebel type. It is inappropriate for people with an Imaginer base who will not take initiatives and who, when managed with this style, risk doing nothing at all.

Table 9.1 Adapting Management Styles to Personality Types

Personality type	Management style to use	Management style to avoid
Harmonizer	Benevolent	Autocratic
Thinker	Democratic	Autocratic
Persister	Democratic	Autocratic
Rebel	Laissez-faire	Autocratic
Imaginer	Autocratic	Laissez-faire
Promoter	Autocratic	Democratic

INDIVIDUALIZED LEADERSHIP

We can see that each of these styles is appropriate for one or two personality types and should be avoided with the others. There is no ideal style, which is something most managers know very well. In the Process Communication Model, we talk of *individualized leadership*. The manager uses the different parts of his or her personality to adopt the appropriate style for each employee: Democratic with people who have a Thinker or Persister base, Autocratic for those with an Imaginer or Promoter base, Laissez-faire with employees who have a Rebel base and Benevolent with those who have a Harmonizer base.

Joan – Oh, I get it. Let the Rebels do as they please and be nice to the Harmonizers.

Peter (frowning) – But if I react differently with each person, they will think it's strange.

Isabelle – You're afraid of not being natural and losing your spontaneity. We also hear that from parents who are told to adapt their behavior to each of their children's temperaments. Still, admit that you intuitively don't behave the same way with each of your employees.

Joan (laughing) – Fortunately.

Jack (quickly) – Knowing the leadership styles helps refine that approach. When everyone feels considered with their unique psychological needs, when the communication style they are addressed in suits them, they aren't frustrated to see that the leader uses another style with a coworker. I overheard someone in the cafeteria this morning saying, "I like my relationship with my manager. I think he understands me. I'm sure that if he acted with me like he does with Frank I wouldn't be able to stand it".

Tom – Sounds to me like manipulation.

Isabelle – Not if you inform everyone…

Joan – Quick get out the trumpet!

Isabelle – No, I mean it. If the manager informs his team on what he has just learned, he can invite them to participate.

Peter (standing and turning to Joan) – Right, but I still need your mock-up for tonight. Absolutely.

Joan – Um, I think you're using the wrong style! (Everyone laughs).

The individualized style is the best way to guarantee each person's motivation. It requires leaders to adapt to each employee's personality, which they already do most of the time, with varying degrees of success. Nonetheless, this approach often involves a deep change for them. In the case of miscommunication, the usual reflex is to demand that the other person change and leaders are like everyone else. Regardless of their adaptive abilities, they often tend to expect their employees to alter their behavior first. "On my team, this is how we do it," is something we often hear. The underlying meaning is, "Fit my mode of functioning."

In the case of relational problems, the "50-50 rule" is much more appropriate for efficient collaboration. Regardless of the origin of the problem or its seriousness, each protagonist is always involved 50-50. Usually this 50-50 rule, which comes from the Palo Alto school, causes heated reactions from our seminar audiences. Each person naturally tends to hold the other person's behavior responsible, which they feel in turn justifies their own behavior. But it is more useful for ourselves and our personal efficiency to ask ourselves, "How did I go about it? How am I responsible for this problem?" than to blame the problem on the other person. As soon as someone realizes their "share" in a problem and decides to change their behavior, the situation immediately changes and it becomes easier to meta-communicate[20]. "The ability to properly meta-communicate, says Paul Watzlawick, "is not just the condition for good communication. It is also closely connected to the vast issue of self-awareness and awareness of others".[21]

However a behavior change in one actor can also cause a problem in reaction. This is the case, for example, of a wife whose husband realizes she has a Harmonizer base and Persister phase and gives her flowers,

---

[20] See page xx

[21] Paul Watzlawick, op. cit.

something he hasn't done in a long while. Instead of a thank-you, she answers suspiciously, "You're not trying to make up for something are you?"

To use the metaphor of a seminar participant, "We have to put our blinker on before making a turn." As managers, it is essential that, after realizing our behavior (and deciding to change) we take the time to explain what we have learned. For instance, for many years a manager only communicates with his Harmonizer Base Persister Phase employee by giving her instructions. On his return from the seminar, he begins to meet her psychological needs by telling her how much he appreciates her. But in fact, he causes suspicion on both sides. "What's behind all this? Why did he say that?" thinks the assistant. And the now suspicious manager thinks, "All those theories we learned were baloney. They don't work in real life".

We all know that when we do not have complete information, we cannot correctly interpret outside events. Real dialogue with employees results in more trust in return, which is a major condition for an efficient organization.

Jack (confiding in Joan) – Now I understand my wife's complaint. Expressing my feelings is as foreign to me as Manhattan is for an Arkansas farmer! I also understand why my secretary asked for a transfer. I really don't know how to interact with people who have a Harmonizer base.

Joan – Explain that to them and things will be better. And stop offering me coffee because of my Rebel base and the fact that I like breaks, you're going to get sick!

THE MANAGER'S PERSONAL DEVELOPMENT PLAN

> *"The boss must become a genuine facilitator. He must be able to trust his subordinates, to help them, to facilitate their task and, through this task, enable them to affirm their personality. That is how he will succeed in mobilizing resources that were unknown to bureaucracy until now."*
>
> Michel Crozier[22]-

---

[22] L'Entreprise à l'écoute, op. cit.

For the manager, using the Process Communication Model involves the desire to change and use his or her new field of knowledge. Corporate culture may limit a manager's ability to change, especially if they are alone in taking this path. Ideally, learning the Process Communication Model will spark a powerful collective desire initiated from the highest level. In any case, this learning results in an action plan that will enable the manager to identify his or her own strong points and areas for improvement.

Let's imagine that a manager is naturally uninclined to use the Laissez-faire style. That is why he encounters difficulties with his Rebel base employees. He believes things should be structured, clear, precise and verifiable (and it is, of course, important that they be so). His improvement strategy will therefore consist in acquiring the characteristics of the Laissez-faire style, in his own way, to progressively become comfortable using this style and be able to manage his staff without "clashing" with them.

This process will require time and attention to his own behavioral habits. For someone used to using the Autocratic style, learning to use a Laissez-faire style can cause some concerns. That is why the manager's personal development is indispensable in order to "become more one's self to be able to effectively and openly engage in the important issues that surround us".[23] Many companies are suspicious of this. They fear the "pressure cooker" syndrome, fearing what will happen when they take off the lid. But this path is not about destabilizing anyone but about progressively enriching the manager's behavioral palette.

Tom – What's all this about personal development? We're not at the shrink's.

Isabelle (shrugging) – You're confusing it. Unlike psychotherapy which consists in untying the knots from our past to free up certain potentials, personal development intervenes on the here and now. People frequently have accessible available potential that they make very little use of. If you want, it's as if they had a building with six apartments. All of them are superb, even if the upper floors are smaller. What's unfortunate is that most of the time they live on the first and second floors. If only they knew that upstairs they had a breathtaking view of the whole city..."

---

[23] Meryem Le Saget, op. cit.

Tom (looking bored) – Yeah…

Anne – If I understand correctly, personally developing one's self means occupying our vital space. But there is still a change in paradigm without which nothing is possible.

Joan – Excuse me?

Anne – Yes. A change in beliefs. Accepting to change one's self before trying to change others and believing that the win-win relationship is really the most effective. Simply because it is much easier to act on our own behavior than on someone else's and easier to cause change in them by being a model than by giving "good advice".

Peter – I would add that the more we understand, the more open we are to change. It is much easier to interact with a distressed Persister type when we are able to identify the phenomenon rather than just thinking the person is a tyrant. Right, Joan?

Joan – Yes, General. (She turns to the others.) I have some good news to announce. Most tyrants are not *real* tyrants. There are unique needs hiding behind their horrible behavior. Except for Peter, where I still have my doubts.

Trainer and Coaches continue to meet in supervision groups to provide support to leaders after the Process Communication Model Seminars.

THE SUPERVISION GROUP

During a supervision group, the leader thinks about his or her practices and learns to develop their leadership effectiveness based on their new reference grid of the Process Communication Model. This group is an aid to change and helps them integrate the model. The same thing happens in Process Communication Model as in tennis. Many people begin learning this sport on their own, until one day they think, "I've reached my level but now I'm stagnating" and they decide to take a course. The first thing they notice immediately afterwards is that they do not play as well as before. There is a regression that precedes integrating the technique and using it naturally. Likewise, after a seminar, leaders have the impression of losing their naturalness in communication and becoming less effective. It's a bit like children who used to crawl across the living room in 4 seconds and take 5 minutes when they learn to walk, with quite of bit of tottering on the way.

The supervision group supports leaders during this integration phase. It starts two or three days after the seminar and takes place every two weeks or once a month. It helps each person develop their agility to access their various personality floors, identify their employees' personality types, solve the leadership problems they encounter, and treat any difficulties with their hierarchy.

Seminar training is customized to each client's need that offers a "package" approach of follow up skill practices. The supervision group optimizes appropriation of this package through personalized support and feedback with other participants.

DECISION-MAKING

Henri Mintzberg[24] classed the manager's activities into three categories: interpersonal relationships, transferring information, and decision-making. We have seen how process management using the Process Communication Model tools can improve managerial effectiveness and the quality of interpersonal relationships.

Given the increasingly complex stakes involved, decision-making requires us to mobilize all of the facets of our personality. The more severe the stress, the harder it is to decide serenely. In cases in which a leader feels "inner conflict" over a problem to solve, the "Tour of the Condo" exercise can prove very useful. This exercise consists in letting each of the parts of ourselves "speak" and listening to what they think, want, or feel about the decision to be made. Ideally we would first ask our base, then the phase, and so on up to the sixth floor of the condominium. The questions are as follows:

Thinker – What factual information do I have to solve this problem?
Persister – What are my values concerning it?
Rebel – What are all the original ideas I can come up with to solve it?
Harmonizer – How do I feel about this problem?
Imaginer – What imaginative possibilities can I discover about it?
Promoter – What can I do immediately to solve it?

---

[24] Cf. Henry Mintzberg, *The Nature of Managerial Work.*

Example:

Carol started her own business that has reached cruising speed. Now she has an opportunity to go into partnership with someone. The decision is an important one. It is a 50-50 business "marriage". Everyone she knows advises against this kind of association. Carol realizes that after a few weeks things are still not completely clear for her. Although she is in Promoter phase and used to forging ahead, she hesitates. Her condominium is as follows: Harmonizer (base) / Promoter (phase) / Rebel / Thinker / Persister / Imaginer. We suggest taking a tour of the condo. Her trip results in the following:

Harmonizer – What I feel is first not wanting to be alone anymore. I feel good with this possible partner, there is no rivalry or negative competition between us. I feel safe. On the other hand, I'm afraid of having to share and change my way of doing things.

Promoter – I want to do business and grow using the relational network, etc. It's an opportunity for me to rapidly double or triple my income.

Rebel – The two of us have strong, independent personalities and for him there is no place for emotion in business and I can't be in partnership with someone without that emotional aspect (recalling the Harmonizer base). One great thing to do would be to each create our own structure and work in synergy. In other words, all the fun and energy but none of the drawbacks. Fantastic!

Thinker – The information I have is as follows: I am used to making decisions on my own; my market is currently in difficulty; having a partner with a high salary could put the company in debt; the option of two structures would let us take our time at little risk.

Persister – What I believe is that, for me, a good partnership is based on good emotional understanding. It's part of my value set. I know that I always give priority to the relational aspect. I cannot conceive of business any other way.

Imaginer – In terms of possibilities, I think that it is important to not overlook the two or three red flags I had on the relational end (this person does not attach a lot of importance to managing the relationship). It is essential to not go onboard if I feel something is holding me back, especially on a project of this importance.

By the end of this exercise, Carol's face relaxed and she smiled. She feels she knows what she wants now, that she can see more clearly into the psychological issues and is more aware of the outside reality. The idea from her Rebel floor suits her and she decides to propose it to her partner.

Another example:

Paul is a business manager. He is a very active member of a big managers association. During a congress he helped organize, he is asked to talk about his own life experience in the gazette that will be handed out on the day of the event. Paul's condominium is as follows: Promoter / Persister (phase) / Thinker / Harmonizer / Imaginer / Rebel. This request causes inner conflict in Paul between the desire for action from his Promoter side and the principles on his Persister side. Here is his condominium tour:

Promoter – It's an exciting project! I would enjoy saying, "Here's what I did, how I seized the opportunities, etc."

Persister – The idea of transmitting something about my convictions appeals to me but I hold the values my father transmitted to me when he said, "Don't put yourself in the spotlight. What counts is what you achieve. Worth is not explained, it is proven. Truly ethical people know how to keep silent."

Thinker – I need more information. What is the objective? Has it already been done? How was it perceived?

Harmonizer – What I feel is fear and also something like "don't try to be important; don't show off".

Imaginer – I'll need time to prepare this article for it to contain certain points on my experience. It's clear that I'm experiencing conflict between the desire to be recognized and the conviction that silence means reliability.

Rebel – It could be fun to tell the story of my company, the originality of the undertaking, its innovative side, etc.

After performing the exercise, Paul feels relaxed. He is surprised at the wealth of different viewpoints and realizes the inner conflict between his taste for action and the reserve his father taught him. He gives himself a little time to think before deciding. In this example, it is interesting to note how the Persister side that reflects his father is a powerful counterweight to his Promoter side. People sometimes see Paul as having a dual personality. He shows both a "plow ahead" side that works on a high level of energy and seeks challenges, and a deep, reserved side that does not seek glory, which are rare characteristics in a person with a Promoter base.

Another example of the roles given to each personality floor, told by a psychotherapist:

> "I have a client who has a Persister side and a Promoter side. He has a very strong critical part which he expresses through his Persister who spends its time inhibiting the Promoter, telling him, "No, you'll never make it. You're not doing anything. You're not working enough. You should work harder." This keeps him from taking action as a Promoter. He has progressively begun to accept himself, to put some positive aspects into his Persister. Today everything is changing for him because he has fully committed to a new project. Now I think he will be able to rely on his Persister to keep the Promoter from going too far too fast."

The "Tour of the Condo" exercise helps us gather precious information on our inner life. It gives us a feeling of relaxation and distance from a situation. It helps us identify any inconsistencies, any conflicts between our different parts and puts us on the path to integrating them better. For instance, we can realize that there is a conflict between a Harmonizer part (seeking company and a warm, relaxed atmosphere) and a Thinker part (putting work ahead of everything). What we feel when we give "everyone a chance to speak" is appeasement, kind of like when each member of a family can express their views on a given point. Of course, this tool is applicable outside of the business world, in all areas of personal life when making a decision is difficult.

TEAM MANAGEMENT

Using the Process Communication Model to manage a team is an in-depth approach that enables the leader to identify the personality type of each employee and the job and environment that suits them best. Next, it involves practicing daily attitudes aimed at satisfying psychological needs. As we have already pointed out, sharing information makes the daily practice of the Process Communication Model much easier.

Peter – About that, I've sometimes wondered whether Process Communication Model could be used to manipulate employees.

Isabelle – The idea of manipulation comes from the idea of dominating others. But the person who feels dominated tends to invest less positive energy into the company and into his or her self. The win-win relationship is more effective. It means, "You're OK, I'm OK". Instead of saying, "I'll use what I've learned to manipulate my employee", it's preferable to say, "We both know what is important in our way of working and relating and we can meta-communicate on what is happening." Ideally, everyone should take a seminar but this is not always possible. But if the manager coming back from a seminar takes the time to explain and dialogue on what he has learned and experienced, and on what he feels should be changed, there is no more risk of manipulation and it becomes relational management.

Anne – It's about always establishing win-win relationships. But the +/+ position isn't natural[25]. It's what Laborit[26] describes when he says that in the living world dominant-dominated relationships are always established, which corresponds to +/- relationships. A lot of energy is spent on gaining ground on the other person, on gaining more power, more advantages, etc. The +/+ position doesn't come naturally and has to be learned.

Jack – That's the whole problem – having to learn and take the time!

Joan – I say that if the manager doesn't take that time, he'll lose it somewhere else.

Anne – In the quicksand of distress.

---

[25]   See life positions page xx

[26]   Henri Laborit, *La Nouvelle Grille*, Robert Lafont, 1985.

Joan – Speaking of fun, I get a charge out of identifying how each of us "betrays" our preferred psychological need. For example, I don't know if you've noticed but our great Thinker, Jack, sometimes remarks on the time he spends on a project, "You know, I worked until 3 a.m." I'd call that an attempt to get recognition for his work. During our little parties when everyone miraculously climbs to their Rebel floor, did you see how Anne crawls into her shell? She seems absent and gazes off as if to say, "I'm not here, let me withdraw". When Isabelle bends over backwards to please and smiles at anyone who looks at her, what is she seeking? Probably to be recognized for who she is.

Isabelle – Okay, that's enough.

Peter – That's not so silly after all.

Joan – Thanks for the compliment, Peter. I would even say it's intelligent. Have you heard how most of your in-house speeches begin? "Ladies and Gentlemen, let's be serious". Isn't that a Persister type looking for recognition? As for our dear Promoter Tom, I noticed that in meetings it doesn't take long for him to start drumming his fingers on the table. A sign that he's boiling with impatience and eager to get into action!

Jack – Someone's missing.

Joan – Who?

Jack – You!

Joan – Oh, yeah.

Jack – Did you see during the Monday morning meeting, when we decide to work for more than 30 minutes without joking, you usually start to wriggle in your seat? You look around the room. In my opinion, you're thinking about how you're going to redecorate your bathroom.

Peter – Or how to use her creativity for a totally other purpose.

Sometimes it takes very little to show an employee that his or her needs are "recognized". The right words and tone already provide the conditions for clear, positive communication. Let's imagine the head of the team at Sofia's & Co. who arrives at the office:

Hello, Jack, congratulations on your report! Could you extract three key ideas from it for tomorrow night? Hello, Peter, I'd like to know your opinion on the best way to reorganize our department. Hi, Joan, so how did your bowling match go last night? What would you say to designing the color animation for our new software? Hey, Tom, go find us three new clients by tomorrow and we'll celebrate! Welcome, Isabelle, how are you? I just heard about your son's success on his exams. Please give him my sincere congratulations. I would be pleased if you took charge of this project that means so much to me on how to improve our customer service[27]. Hello, Anne, please take charge of the in-depth analysis of our key sources of dysfunction like we defined yesterday.

In this example of motivational strategy used by the Sofia's & Co. manager, we strive towards what Martin Bubber[28] calls "real humanity". "The basis of life of man with man is double and at the same time unique. Man's desire to be confirmed in what he is and can become by other men, and man's innate ability to respond to this desire in his human companions. That this ability lies fallow to an unimaginable degree is the weakness and effective problem of the human species. Real humanity only exists where this ability can develop."

TRANSFER EFFECT

A leader is a natural transfer medium. In other words, many employees see them as paternal figures. Unconsciously, many things will be played out between a team member and a team leader depending on each person's history. The other is no longer the other but the person they recall from our history. This is what we call the transfer effect.

> Alan does not understand why he feels positive or negative feelings towards people he doesn't know. It is probable that something is unconsciously playing out and that these people remind Alan of other people he knew in the past and for whom he felt those same feelings. Let's imagine that he had very conflictual relationship with his father. If the manager has some of the man's characteristics, it is probably that when Alan is in distress that he tends to replay that script. He might inwardly say to the manager, "I'm very intimidated by you" or "I always feel at fault when I'm with

---

[27] Someone with a Thinker base will probably note that the interaction with Isabelle lasts twice as long as with the others. It would be an exaggeration to deduce that it is more time consuming to manage an employee with a Harmonizer base than another personality type.

[28] Cited by Paul Watzlawick in *Pragmatics of Communication*, op. cit.

you." In those moments, he projects a paternal figure he experienced as repressive onto his manager.

Transfer is one aspect of the relationship that all leaders should be aware of and understand its importance. Using the inappropriate communication channel can activate this transfer mechanism. It will not be a matter of the leader treating this phenomenon related to the employee's history, but of monitoring the quality of the relationship and communication in order to avoid its emergence.

TRANSFER AND MASKS

Second degree masks are sometimes due to transfer effects.

When he was a child, Alan integrated an Attacker mask from his father. When his manager uses a Directive channel with him, Alan may not receive this channel and instead hear the paternal Attacker mask that, on conditioned reflex, triggers his own second degree mask. In this case he will have archaic reactions like, "I'm incapable", or "He can try all he wants, I'm not going to be pushed around", etc.

The more information a manager has to understand behaviors, the more he knows what the needs are, the easier it will be to adapt rather than think, "What's wrong with this one again?" No one expects a manager to be a psychologist. It is not their role, however they can manage the process to avoid this kind of phenomenon. If two people who are communicating are thinking clearly, there cannot be a transfer because they are both in the here and now and not back then and somewhere else.

Let's take the case of someone who transfers a repressive parental figure onto a manager and wears a Drooper or Blamer mask. If the manager responds by attacking, he reproduces the other person's childhood script and we come full circle. The person has the unconscious confirmation that "it's always the same thing". However, if the manager responds appropriately to the person on the Emotive or Nurturative channel, the past script is no longer fueled and they experience a "different" reality. Unfortunately, masks invite masks and that is what usually causes escalation.

Andrew runs an insurance office in a small town. He spends most of his time with the clientele and has recently fired his Harmonizer base secretary who had been unable to assume her duties for a while. Shortly after firing her, he took part in a Process Communication Model seminar and discovered that he has a Thinker base and is currently in Promoter phase. He realizes that part of the difficulties with his secretary were due to his phase. He tended to expect her to get along on her own and had not supported her enough in her new tasks as his business quickly grew. To recruit a new assistant, he decides not to hire someone with the same profile (he is aware that he has trouble supporting them), nor with a Rebel profile (his natural Autocratic management style tends to "get their dander up"). So he recruits an employee with a Persister base in a Thinker phase who seems very self-sufficient. A few months later, this assistant sometimes has reactions that correspond to the Rebel type in distress. The manager does not understand this and the two begin having relational problems. Andrew proposes that his employee also take part in a Process Communication Model seminar.

She is enthusiastic when she returns. "I've understood something fundamental for me about the transfer effect," she explains to Andrew. "I realized that every time you show me your "hard Promoter", I feel stubborn and react negatively. Well, my older brother has a Promoter base. When we were kids he was always the darling and our dad's favorite. I revolted against that favoritism. I realize that when you show the same kind of attitude as my brother, I tend to have very strong reactions – like back then".

Andrew now understands the deeper meaning of their relational difficulties and shows his understanding. Together they decide to meta-communicate if this kind of situation reoccurs. Andrew also realizes how sensitive he is to aggressiveness from a woman which is probably also due to a transfer for him.

PSYCHOLOGICAL TRADING STAMPS

Eric Berne[29] developed the concept of psychological trading stamps in reference to the former commercial practice of receiving trading stamps for what we bought when we went shopping. The more we bought, the more stamps we got, which we would take home and stick

---

[29]   Eric Berne, op. cit.

in a book. When the book was full we could go and cash it in for a gift. The bigger the stamp collection, the bigger the gift.

The analogy with trading stamps is easy to make for situations in which, for example, people "take it" without saying anything. We say they are "collecting their stamps".

-   Okay, you did that to me. It's doesn't matter but I won't forget.
-   I'm the specialist and they didn't consult me. It's clear, I see what this means.
-   I didn't get a raise this year. Are they ever going to pay for it!

These reactions correspond to filling the stamp book. When the person feels that the book is full, they are entitled to the "right psychological gift".

-   I was right to fire him after everything he did!
-   If that's how it is, then I'm taking a week's sick leave.
-   In that case, it will be a pleasure to trip him up when he least expects it.

Psychological trading stamps are among the biggest polluters in a relationship. The bigger the stamp book between two people, the more they are in miscommunication. The more this miscommunication increases, the more the stamp book grows and so on. The relationship is imprisoned in a vicious circle.

The manager's strategy will be to encourage the members of his or her team to trade stamps. How? Not by getting even – which would fatten the book even more – but by establishing the relationship and being listened to and heard in terms of each person's needs. For instance, we can learn to say, "I was frustrated when you gave that task to someone else", or "This is what I felt about that". If the person receives these remarks by showing openness and understanding, we feel relief and the relationship is reinforced, which will restore trust. "Now I know that it is really possible to say what's wrong without risking retaliation," concluded an employee with a very full book at the end of a team seminar.

However, trading in our stamps is no more natural than communicating in the +/+ position. It requires willingness and overcoming strong reticence, followed by training and practice, during seminars for example. For many people, saying things the way they are is difficult and unusual. "I don't know how to say what's wrong in a positive way." It often requires support at first. This new "culture" helps progressively erase the anxiety of the "pressure cooker syndrome" ("I better not open it or it will explode") and enables us to realize how much this way of operating frees up energy (collecting trading stamps consumes a tremendous amount of it).

Working as a team with a moderator helps differentiate between someone "evening the score", complete with second degree masks, and trading stamps. Afterwards, the team can schedule regular dialogue meetings. The group no longer feels like a "snake pit" but simply a group of people who work together and express their feelings. This approach always results in a positive outcome in terms of the relational quality of a group and therefore its efficiency, as long as the process is managed positively, of course.

TEAM COHESION

Another area in which the Process Communication Model is a powerful business tool is team cohesion. It is the most efficient means of sharing information, as well as raising awareness of the team's structure and its performance opportunities. It affects us on several levels:

- Better knowledge of ourselves, our psychological needs, and stress management techniques
- Better knowledge of the other team members
- Learning a common language for daily communication and conflict management
- Defining the team profile and an action and development plan that takes each person's strong points and improvement areas into account

The entire project requires training with the team and its manager. It is based on personality inventories for each participant. During the training, the team discovers three fundamental concepts for understanding its mode of functioning, its internal communication and the processes that lead to conflict. These concepts are the team profile, conflict dynamics, and the interaction pattern.

Joan – Excuse me?

Jack – The interaction pattern. Each person puts in the personality types for which they have at least 60% of their energy, in other words, the ones they can easily mobilize to communicate (see table 9.2).

Joan – Okay, our base and maybe our phase.

Jack (slightly irritated) – No. *All* of the types for which we have at least 60% available energy. It can be the case for three or four floors of our condominium. Once each person has put their types on a spreadsheet using color codes by type. It is easy to see any relational difficulties.

Isabelle – Let's say a person most easily uses their energy in Harmonizer and Rebel and works with someone every day who feels most comfortable on the Imaginer and Promoter floors. It is probable that they have some difficulty understanding each other. The mere fact of benefiting from a description of the interaction problems helps relieve any tension and enables them to talk about the relationship. One could say, "I would have liked to have had warmer contact with you." and the other, "It didn't occur to me. My reflex is to plow on ahead." Using Process Communication Model works like a mediator and "neutralizes" any value judgements.

Anne – We could say that the interaction pattern helps us understand the natural forces that exist within the team and gives us a different outlook on the relational "knots" inherent to any system.

This approach also helps imagine how each person's psychological needs can be satisfied. Let's take the example of a team composed of members whose base is either Thinker or Persister with one member who has a Rebel base and is in Imaginer phase. It is probable that this person feels about as comfortable as a bull in a china shop and has difficulty functioning with the others. During a seminar, the entire team thinks about this situation in order to enrich its efficiency based on this specificity. The prerequisite is to accept people's differences. But this is much easier to do once these are understood (especially for the Thinker and Persister types who need to understand in order to act).

As an illustration, let's take a team composed of Frank, Kathy, David, Claudine, and Anthony. The team's interaction pattern will be represented based on each person's profile.

Table 9.1: Interaction Patterns Based on Individual Profiles

	Persister	Rebel	Thinker	Promoter	Harmonizer	Imaginer
Frank	100	80	55	40	35	25
Kathy	50	45	75	20	100	30
David	45	85	50	40	55	100
Claudine	45	20	100	65	50	30
Anthony	100	40	100	35	75	30
Total	340	270	380	200	315	215
Average (total: 5)	68	54	76	40	63	43

Frank, Kathy, Claudine, and Anthony can easily communicate from their Thinker and Persister floors. Since David only shares the Rebel part with Frank, he will need to maintain a high level of energy to adapt to his team's dominant functioning mode (does the group accept his natural tendency towards playfulness and does it use his creativity?) The Promoter part in Claudine probably does not encounter much recognition from the rest of the team.

Now the team has the necessary information for drafting its personality structure. This corresponds to the mathematical average of the components of each member. The profile we obtain has the advantage of being simple and immediately operational (figure 9.2).

Figure 9.2: Team Profile

Thinker 76	Persister 68	Harmonizer 63	Rebel 54	Imaginer 43	Promoter 40

Joan – We're the ideal team. The comprehensive product, guaranteed 100% of each type. We ought to be running the government!

Jack – Ideal? That depends for whom.

Peter – If I understand it, the structure of management teams is often: Persister / Thinker / Harmonizer / Rebel / Imaginer / Promoter. They have a lot of energy on the first two floors and not much energy on the last two or three. Their strengths: "Thinker" professionalism, a sense of management, organization, and planning, with "Persister" high moral standards and tenacity. Their areas for improvement: listening (also a "Persister" syndrome), the search for certainty and pickiness ("Thinker" tendency), little concern for people (lack Harmonizer traits), little creativity, difficulty adapting and not enough in-depth thought – due to a lack of time, naturally.

Isabelle – They can derive an action plan from this profile. They can realize how they need to develop to optimize their resources. They could select actions to improve their weak points. For example:

> At one of our recent seminars, the composition of a management team reflected the profile described above. The different bases and phases of this team were as follows: Persister/Harmonizer, Persister/Promoter, Thinker/Persister, Persister/Rebel, Thinker/Harmonizer, Persister/Thinker. Here is the reaction from the participants:

> "This profile made us think a lot. Our team knows how to analyze problems and summarize them but it is weaker when it comes to action. We need to be attentive to this aspect. Especially since the only member with a strong focus on action is in Promoter phase, but... he goes much too fast. We have to set up monitoring systems that would guarantee a better division of resources."

Just like for the leadership styles, a team's ability to integrate the Process Communication Model represents substantial time savings. We sometimes hear managers say, "In our company, 40% of our energy is spent on communication." And we also hear the employees add, "Oh, if only it were just 40%!"

Yet, nothing is "magic" about this. Power struggles do not disappear overnight. It is just that now the antagonists have a tool to manage them in a healthy way if they decide to use it. The leader must ensure that the method is sustained and maintained. It is the manager's own commitment that enables the other changes. The more a management team takes care to answer the psychological needs of its members, the more those members will be able to do the same thing with their teams. However, if the leader causes them distress, they will also tend to pass that distress onto their subordinates.

Miscommunication is the key risk that threatens a team. It leads to frustration, discontent, low energy and conflictual situations. A team's success or failure largely depends on the resources it has to optimize the quality of its relationships. The simpler, more personalized, more known to everyone the relationships are, the more they guarantee team efficiency.

One of the immediate benefits of this training for a team is discovering the importance of meta-communication. One of the exercises participants enjoy most is the one in which each person says what they like and do not like in a coworker's behavior. A frequent conclusion from these feedback sessions is, "We've worked together for over ten years and didn't know each other."

After a seminar, a participant gave us the following feedback: "During the seminar, one of us was revealed as being in Harmonizer phase and that surprised us a lot because he never showed it. The fact of discovering it enabled him to open up more and be considered differently with a positive impact on our relationship."

The usual reluctance towards saying what we think and feel comes from an often explicit fear of "backlash" and from cultural pressure that demands a lot of restraint in this area.

Yet, this kind of exercise is precious since it provides information on how each individual is perceived, their strong points (often unknown), and areas for improvement (also sometimes unknown or exaggerated). It also helps participants to reach a very high level of energy and self-confidence and creates a clear reinforcement of team cohesion. Of course the moderator's role is fundamental for this kind of exercise. The moderator must ensure an atmosphere of acceptance, kindness and authenticity.

Team cohesion training provides both personalized tools and references for the group. It also enables the emergence of a common language. During a conflict, an uninvolved member can press the alarm button and say, "Can we talk a minute about what's happening?" and invite the others to decode the conflictual situation in the Process Communication Model.

TEAM CONFLICT DYNAMICS

When the psychological needs are not satisfied in a team, predictable conflict issues will arise as an attempt by people to negatively satisfy their needs. The large majority of conflict between the members of a team are due to the fact that one of them did not obtain what they wanted. The

KAHLER COMMUNICATIONS, INC.

degree of conflict tells us the extent of the distress this person is in and how it affects their job. It also tells us which strategy to use to intervene and help the team resolve this conflict. Like a chain that is as strong as its weakest link, a team has the efficiency of its most distressed member.

In the event of conflict, the first thing to do is identify the origins, decode the meaning by analyzing the negative mechanism that has been triggered and give it the appropriate response. This means answering the underlying need positively and returning to positive communication on the right communication channel.

Each personality type has three degrees of visible conflict.

Harmonizer Type in Conflict within the Team

In first degree miscommunication, the Harmonizer type thinks that the team will accept them if they please. They then begin to give responses that are of no interest to the job but are attempts to be accepted and appreciated. In second degree, the employee wears a Drooper mask and makes mistakes that cause the team to criticize them. If the person goes all the way to third degree miscommunication, they could be rejected by the team, get fired for errors, with the deep conviction that no one loves them. Unconsciously the person can even cause unconditional rejection.

Table 9.3: Conflict Dynamics for the Harmonizer Type

1st degree	Please You	I'm doing everything I can to please you.
2nd degree	Drooper	I'm an idiot. I didn't understand.
3rd degree	Despairer	It's too rough. I'm at my limit. I can't take it anymore.

Thinker Type in Conflict within the Team

The Thinker type in first degree miscommunication operates from a Be Perfect for you driver. They over-detail, think for others, and have trouble delegating since they are convinced that they can do better, faster and more efficiently than the others.

If they move into second degree miscommunication, they wear an Attacker mask and their behavior shows anger, frustration and criticism. They over-control and feel frustrated by the members of the team who do not accept their ideas. They verbally attack subordinates who "don't think", criticize team members on hours, fairness, responsibility, orderliness, or work. If they enter into third degree miscommunication Thinker type personalities convince themselves there is no point in staying with people who don't know how to solve problems. They reject the team and its members on the excuse that they are stupid or incompetent.

Table 9.4: Conflict Dynamics for the Thinker Type

1st degree	Be Perfect for you	I'll do it myself. It's safer.
2nd degree	Attacker	Show me how far you've gotten. Do it like this. Are you stupid or what?
3rd degree	Despairer	They're all inept. What would we do without me? I can't count on anyone here.

Persister Type in Conflict within the Team

In first degree miscommunication, the Persister type employee wears a Be Perfect for me mask. This type expects as much dedication, loyalty, and hard work as they deliver themselves, and focuses on what is wrong, not seeing what is right.

In second degree miscommunication, they wear an Attacker mask and feel righteous anger. They reject members of the team who do not accept their opinions and they crusade. They tend to verbally attack anyone who does not seem committed enough. They are critical and suspicious of people who do not believe in the "cause". Lastly, in third degree, the Persister type feels deep frustration. "If you're not with me, you're against me". They could ultimately abandon the team, convinced that it is disloyal or that "they have no values".

Table 9.5: Conflict Dynamics for the Persister Type

1st degree	Be Perfect for me	Your conclusion lacks meaning. You are wrong. It's not THAT bad of an idea.
2nd degree	Attacker	Prove what you are saying. So the company doesn't matter to you, is that it? I've asked you 100 times to set higher standards. I speak English, don't I?
3rd degree	Despairer	They're all in cahoots against me!

Imaginer Type in Conflict within the Team

In first degree distress, employees with an Imaginer base form their "be strong" driver. They will therefore protect themselves by integrating with the team as little as possible and becoming passive. In second degree miscommunication, they wear a Drooper mask and feel uncomfortable, like misfits. Characteristic behavior of this degree for the Imaginer type is to begin several projects without finishing them. Lastly, convinced of being neglected and unwanted (existential question: Am I wanted?), they manage to stay in a corner and be totally ignored by the team. "No one told me what to do!"

Table 9.6: Conflict Dynamics for the Imaginer Type

1st degree	Be Strong for you	People are making too much noise. I'm crawling into my shell.
2nd degree	Drooper	I feel remote from all this. I'm uncomfortable. I don't know how. I don't have enough time.
3rd degree	Despairer	I'm all alone. No one speaks to me. I don't know what to do anymore.

Rebel Type in Conflict within the Team

When Rebel type employees drift into miscommunication, they try harder. They will show that they do not understand and invite the other team members to do or think in their place. "I don't understand what you're asking me." Or "I don't know how to do that."

In second degree miscommunication, this personality type upsets the team, blames, complains, splits hairs, accuses others, refuses to admit to their mistakes and generally disturbs things. If we let this type drift into third degree miscommunication, they disapprove and contradict in a vindictive spirit that can result in them becoming totally excluded by the team members and breaking off relations in a spirit of revenge. "You'll pay for this!"

Table 9.7: Conflict Dynamics for the Rebel Type

1st degree		I can't do it. It's too hard. I don't understand. I don't know how.
	Try Hard for you	
2nd degree		What report? It's not my fault if it isn't finished. I've had it! You're always on my back.
	Blamer	
3rd degree		You just wait and see. You're going to pay for this!
	Despairer	

Promoter Type in Conflict within the Team

The Promoter type behaves as though the team members have to "be strong" if they want to be on the same team as him or her. They expect everyone to manage on their own and do not support their coworkers or subordinates. In second degree miscommunication, this type feels trapped and becomes vindictive. They blame and try to "get back" at others. They tend to manipulate, to pit the members of the team against one another, create conflict within the team or try to fool its members. They take an overall attitude meant to show that they are special and entitled to "special status". Lastly, in third degree miscommunication, this type will react with disdain, considering that the others are incapable. Promoter type personalities will abandon the team and its members before the team abandons them.

Table 9.8: Conflict Dynamics for the Promoter Type

1st degree	Be Strong for me	Here it's each man for himself. It's not my problem. Figure it out for yourself.
2nd degree	Blamer	If you didn't get a raise this year it's because of Peter. Do you realize who you're talking to? Did you hear what he said about you?
3rd degree	Despairer	I give your company six months before it falls apart at the seams! They're all losers!

Table 9.9: Three Degrees of Conflict and the Six Personality Types

Personality types	First degree	Second degree	Third degree
Harmonizer	Attempts to please. Over-adapts to others. Doesn't ask directly for things.	Makes mistakes. Invites criticism.	Is rejected: "I could tell they didn't love me."
Thinker	Expects self to be perfect. Has trouble delegating: "I can do it better and faster than the others."	Over-controls. Becomes frustratedly angry.	Reject the team: "They're all stupid."
Persister	Expects perfection from others. Focuses on what is wrong.	Crusades. Becomes suspicious. Tries to impose their views.	Abandons the team. "They have no commitment"
Imaginer	Expects self to be strong. Withdraws and spins wheels.	Waits passively.	Is ignored by the team. "No one told me what I was supposed to do."
Rebel	Tries hard. Won't understand. Invites others to think and do for them.	Blames. Rejects responsibility. Becomes vengeful	Is agitated. Is censured by others.
Promoter	Expects others to be strong. Does not support coworkers when they have difficulties. "It's each man for himself."	Manipulates. Creates tension within the team. Becomes vindictive.	Abandons the others before the others can abandon them.

CHAPTER 10

THE PROCESS COMMUNICATION MODEL IN SALES

Even more critical than in a management situation, the quality of relationships is fundamental to a successful sales situation. While a manager can improve a relationship that gets off to a bad start, in sales there is "no room for error" because a client who is frustrated in the sales relationship is rarely inclined to give the salesperson a second chance.

At a time when the intrinsic quality of products, their cost, and their reliability are increasingly similar across the competition, the quality of the relationship established by the salesperson with the prospect or client determines the potential of a successful conclusion. The salesperson has the best chance of achieving his or her goal if they first adapt to the client, create contact, listen, consider the client's needs, and make an offer that meets the demand, while treating any objections firmly and serenely, concluding with a win-win position.

It is rare for all of these basic qualities to exist in one person. However, they can be developed, in particular by knowing and using the Process Communication Model. The approach offers two essential benefits:

- It helps salespeople manage the client relationship based on the client's sources of motivation and helps them use the right communication channel.
- It teaches salespeople to be aware of their own energy levels by learning their own psychological needs and distress signals. Once they are "charged" with positive energy, they are fully able to adapt and be more flexible in managing their relationships.

The overall strategy for a sales situation is the same as for management. It first involves making a diagnosis and then using the three sources of motivation: psychological needs, communication channels, and client perceptions.

Many buying situations can invite stress in a client, for whatever reason. We will see below how the client shows distress depending on their personality type and what the appropriate responses should be for the salesperson.

Lastly, since the sales situation is often a source of stress for many salespeople as well, we will see how each personality type shows distress and how to manage it.

During a seminar, when a salesperson discovers his or her own personality structure, they realize why they naturally feel more in sync with certain clients, while with others the negotiation can seem like a lost cause. For example, if a salesperson has a Persister base in Thinker phase (many technical salespeople have this profile), negotiations naturally seem easier with prospects who have the same personality structure. On the other hand, the salesperson has less energy for Harmonizer and Rebel types who are at the top of his condominium. Salespeople know how negotiation sessions with clients who have these characteristics can be a source of stress that cost a lot of energy and can sometimes fail.

The sales manager of an automobile dealership who had trained in the Process Communication Model observed that the average length of a sales meeting was two to three times longer with a client who had the same characteristics as the salesperson and that the client/sales ratio varied in the same proportions. The manager conducted his survey by interviewing his sales staff and asking them to describe the day's clients. He made his determination based on these descriptions.

The descriptions the sales staff made of their clients were important because, the more they described positive traits that were similar to their own, the more the description indicated that they felt in sync with their clients and vice versa.

Joan – That's funny. It reminds of when I called the plumber and he recommended a water softener and sent me a specialist. The specialist ploughed in head-on with, "But, Ma'am, I don't understand why your installer didn't make you get a softener!" So I immediately shot back, "Dude, nobody makes me do anything."

Tom – It reminds me of a story, too. I wanted to change cars and I looked into the terms I could get in Boston. I went to the local dealer who had a car I really liked. I told the sales guy, "In Boston they're offering me 10% off. Can you keep up with that?" He answered, "Sir, here we don't have to keep up with anyone." He gave me a whole speech in negative Persister mode. That clashed with me and I turned the relationship into a challenge like, "You're showing resistance and I like that. We'll see who wins." I was about to slam the door in his face and leave.

Isabelle – When I bought my car, the salesperson – who was just charming – offered to deliver it to my home. On delivery day he said, "I'll call you in a month to see if you're satisfied." And he did! I was very sensitive to that show of attention. Next time I need a new car I'll go back to see him.

Joan – Well, you sure are lucky. I bought a cute little car and the sales guy warned me to fill the tank when I left the dealership and I ran out of gas before I even made it to the gas station.

Anne – What you are saying is interesting. When I had to change my car I felt intruded upon by a salesperson who kept joking all the time. I left with an uncomfortable feeling and without making a decision. I went to another dealership outside of town and met a salesperson who was much calmer. I felt comfortable with him and bought my car from him.

Jack – Your stories show once again how we are all different. Personally, I have never bought a car without looking at all the dealerships and I always make my decision at home after studying and comparing all the literature I can find. I've never let myself be influenced by a salesperson.

Peter – For me, I've bought the same make of car for the last 25 years and from the same salesperson!

CLIENT IDENTIFICATION

All salespeople know how the first seconds of initial contact are crucial to the quality of the sales relationship. This relationship will not be established the same way with a client who has a Harmonizer, Thinker, or Promoter base, etc. To ensure this, a salesperson who is familiar with the Process Communication Model observes what is happening in order to adapt to what the client shows him. For example, he notes whether the client shows impatience concerning time, if she is often interrupted, if she mainly asks questions to seek information (Thinker); if he needs to talk about himself, his values, his achievements, the history of the company (Persister). Or is it someone who begins by establishing the relationship with the salesperson by taking care of them, offering coffee, asking whether the trip went well, etc. (Harmonizer) or do they first try to joke a bit (Rebel) or is the client someone who seeks challenge and immediately invites the salesperson into competition (Promoter) or, the opposite, is it someone who speaks very little and makes little contact (Imaginer). The salesperson notes the first signals the prospect or client shows to indicate their base. These few seconds of observation provide precious information to guide the diagnosis. Below are the main tendencies for each personality type in terms of how they enter into a relationship and their basic sources of motivation.

Harmonizer Type: Here is a very caring person

The client with a Harmonizer base approaches the sales rep with a smile. She warmly shakes hands, asks the rep how he is and seeks personal information. "Are you married? Do you have children?" Or she tells him about her own personal life and listens closely to him (especially if the sales rep is warm). This client profile can be self-deprecating, "You know, I don't know a thing", or seem intimidated by what the salesperson says.

Clients with Harmonizer base prefer working with someone who recognizes them as individuals and who wants to establish a warm, personalized relationship. Trying to rush them is the best way to confuse them, which is never a good thing for a salesperson. They like to be called by name, even by their first name. They appreciate sincere compliments and lunches in pleasant venues. When appropriate, small gifts that involve the senses are welcome (coffee, tea, chocolate, cold drinks, flowers, fine wines and even a good cigar for those who enjoy them).

Psychological needs: recognition of person / satisfaction of sensory needs

Thinker Type: He is a professional

The Thinker type person usually gets right to the point. They know what they want, seek information, and often have good knowledge of the products on the market. The style of contact is serious and seeks to evaluate the salesperson's professionalism. Clients with this personality type often refer to their jobs, their skills or their company and do not try to establish personal relations.

These clients like to do business with someone who knows what they are talking about, who fully prepares their meetings and arrives armed with facts and useful data. A good way to form an alliance is by giving them all the necessary information in record time. They appreciate signs of recognition of their competence and their business achievements. They like to make their own decisions and be solicited for their ideas.

Psychological needs: recognition for their work and time structure

Persister Type: Here is someone I can trust!

The client with a Persister base observes attentively, looking straight into the salesperson's eyes as if to evaluate him. This type can seem suspicious or not very open. They search for references concerning reliability, duration, investment, safety, etc. They smile little and immediately express judgements on the products or services being offered. They try to assess whether they can trust the salesperson because they will only do business with someone they trust, with whom they have established mutual respect. They want to be informed with integrity and professionalism. Any confrontation on what is right or appropriate does not have its place here. Clients with a Persister base need time… to give their trust.

Psychological needs: recognition of work/convictions

Imaginer Type: I'll think about it!

The client with an Imaginer base is usually a bit withdrawn and sometimes does not know what to say. They do not seek long discussions and answer the salesperson's questions briefly. They interact little and can seem undecided or even uninterested. They prefer to be alone as soon as possible and do not particularly want to chat or develop friendly relations with the salesperson. Salespeople should be prepared to be straightforward and concise and probably take the initiative. They can offer suggestions or opinions but as briefly and concretely as possible with no joking or attempts to establish personal relations. For example, the cozy little restaurant is inappropriate for the Imaginer type.

Psychological needs: solitude and directives

Promoter Type: What do I get out of it?

The client with a Promoter base gets straight to the point and proposes challenges. "Your competitor is giving me 10%. Can you beat that?" This type is more interested in appearances and in what the salesperson "shows off" than in technical information. This type tends to be impatient and wants the product or service immediately. They try to negotiate tooth and nail and do not hesitate to use challenges or the "hot and cold treatment". They love ultimatums: "Take it or leave it."

Clients with a Promoter personality type usually function on the register of action. "How is it new and how much will it earn me quickly?" Once they decide to buy, they often want to conclude right away and have the product delivered immediately. They enjoy making good deals and tend to have a short-term view that aims at the essential. They prefer doing business with someone stimulating who offers them unique opportunities and shares their sense of challenge. It is possible to get straight to the point with these clients without offending them. Details and flowery compliments tend to bore them.

Psychological needs: excitement

Rebel Type: You're a hoot

The client with a Rebel base likes good times and laughter. They can't stand anyone who takes themselves seriously. They try to establish "buddy" relationships with the salesperson. They like to call each other by their first names and chat about cool things in life. "Where can you get some fun around here?" They seek little technical information (except if they are passionate about the topic) but more originality, gadgets, and a laid-back, friendly atmosphere in the relationship with the salesperson. As soon as we are "pals" with this type, they will not check out the competition.

The Rebel type client prefers doing business with "fun" people and companies. Getting straight to the point could seem boring and non-motivating to these profiles. They expect positive, lively contact from the salesperson and appreciate being invited out to lunch or to parties. It is possible to call them spontaneously for a new idea or new product or service. They will probably decide quickly. Trying to lead them where they do not want to go would be a mistake. They will detect it and immediately react to anything resembling manipulation.

Psychological needs: contact

MASTERING THE ART OF SALES

Once the salesperson has identified his or her prospect's phase, they know what psychological needs must be satisfied in the relationship. The art of sales consists in handling this delicate alchemy of the relationship between two or several individuals, while avoiding the ever-present dangers of manipulation. Here is an example of how the model is used that was given to us by a sales rep for a catering company who explains the difference he makes between manipulation and the +/+ position.

"Our sales folks are all great manipulators. It's a known fact. Yet our clients are not really manipulated. We have good relationships with them that are as transparent as possible. That's what distinguishes us from our competitors today. We have even sent some of our clients to learn the Process Communication Model! Once they are familiar with the tools we use, it can only be a win-win."

Being able to immediately meet the psychological needs the client shows guarantees that client's openness and motivation.

Client Communication Channels

After identifying the client's base, the salesperson will use the client's preferred communication channel to communicate. In this case there is every chance that the client will feel "in sync" and motivated to do business together. On the other hand, if the salesperson offers the client an inappropriate communication channel, the client could put on a mask and fall into miscommunication.

Table 10.1: Using the Right Communication Channel

Client	Communication channel	Examples
Harmonizer	Nurturative	It's so great to have you in the store again
Thinker	Requestive	May I give you the technical features?
Persister	Requestive	What do you believe is important concerning this product?
Imaginer	Directive	Give us your instructions. We will follow them to the letter. Please explain what you mean by that. Give me forty-eight hours and I'll get back to you.
Promoter	Directive	Describe the product you are looking for. Take a look at those colors. Tell me if this exceptional offer interests you.
Rebel	Emotive	.Awesome! They really rock!

Client Perceptions

We have seen that each personality type tends to see the world (and therefore salespeople and their products) based on one key perception. The Persister type perceives the world through his or her opinions; Thinker through thought and facts; Harmonizer through emotions; Rebel in reaction (love it or hate it); Promoter through action and Imaginer through inaction or reflection (does not take the initiative).

We can identify the client perceptions by the verbs, words, and expressions they use to communicate. Along with the psychological needs and communication channels, using these perceptions is an essential source of connection and motivation. And, vice versa, speaking a language the client does not hear will lead straight to failed negotiations. Table 10.2 provides some example of words that indicate each type's preferred perception. Listening to the client's perception is also a precious tool for diagnosing their base.

Table 10.2: Identifying the Personality Type Based on the Client's Words

Personality type	Perception	Verbs, words, expressions
Harmonizer	Emotions	Feeling, senses, being touched, sensitive, warm, harmonious, soft, happy, sad, desire, like, close, fear, scary, appeal
Persister	Opinions	Believe, trust, reliability, investment, loyalty, quality, courage, judge, good, bad, appropriate, you are right/wrong.
Thinker	Thought	Think, count, understand, know, experiment, fair, true, false, information, facts, measures, characteristics, data, evaluate, measure, deadline, cost, guarantee, compare, objectives
Imaginer	Inaction /reflection	Wait, listen, consider, imagine, reflect, undecided, calm, quiet, peace, take time, solitude
Rebel	Reactions	Great, I love it, I hate it, want, fun, ho-hum, play, gadget, original, hip, totally in. Plus an entire range of onomatopoeia.
Promoter	Actions	Head-on, straight to the point, challenge, bottom line, net/net, right now, showy, terms, fashion, benefits, excite, go for it, Bet you can't.

Client in Distress

When their psychological needs are unsatisfied or the communication channel is inappropriate, the client will become distressed and display a driver[30] behavior. Here are some examples of manifestations of drivers for each personality type and the response from the salesperson who is on the right communication channel.

HARMONIZER = Please You / Observable Behavior: Over-adapts, Self-doubt

Examples:

Client – This may be a stupid question but what is this button for?

Salesperson (in an encouraging, understanding tone) – I'm happy to help you. This button is for...

Client – Could you maybe explain the difference between these two models?

Salesperson (with a warm smile) – It's a pleasure Assisting you. This model is for...

Client – I don't know what to choose. I can't make up my mind.

Salesperson (in a reassuring tone) – I feel you need some time. I'm glad to help you.

THINKER = Be Perfect for You / Observable Behavior: Over-details, "splits hairs"

Examples:

Client – I'm not sure I have all of the necessary information about this product.

Salesperson – What other information do you need?

Client – It's about the exact amount of the monthly installments and I wonder how long, I mean...

Salesperson – For a 12-month loan, monthly installments including insurance are...

Client – I don't have much time to give you.

Salesperson – How much time do you have? I'll be brief.

---

[30]   See definition page xx

PERSISTER = Be Perfect for Me / Observable Behavior: Asks complicated questions, focuses on what's wrong

Examples:

Client – Will you show me exactly what the key advantages of this updated model are.

Salesperson – What are you most concerned with?

Client – What is this habit of importing parts? We're in America, aren't we?

Salesperson – I understand your concern. Would you like me to explain the technical reasons for this?

Client – What are your product's features and the key advantages it has over the same product from the competition and what warranty you can offer me.

Salesperson – What do you believe is most important?

IMAGINER = Be Strong / Observable Behavior: Little interaction, tends to withdraw

Examples:

Client – I would like some information on delivery.

Salesperson – Sign here and your order will be delivered in a week.

Client – I don't know how to decide.

Salesperson – Tell me which features you imagine are necessary.

Client – All this paperwork seems complicated.

Salesperson –Show me what's confusing you.

PROMOTER = Be Strong for Me / Observable Behavior: Says "you" when meaning "I", invites other to think they are not in charge of their emotions or thoughts, expects others to fend for themselves

Examples:

Client – What made you think that discount would be enough?

Salesperson – Tell me what will work.(With a wink that says, "We get each other.")

Client – You know how you're looking for a deal and you just can't make it happen?

Salesperson (in a straightforward, stimulating tone) – Show me the terms that make it happen.

Client – You don't need my guidance. Figure it out.

Salesperson – Tell me what you'd do.

REBEL = Try Hard / Observable Behavior: "I can't understand", invites the salesperson to "work"

Examples:

Client – I didn't understand a word of your explanation.

Salesperson (with a wink and a smile) – I hate it when that happens!

Client (laborious tone) – I'd like to know about, um, the difference between, between... these products.

Salesperson (with a knowing smile) – Sweet! I'd love to show you.

Client – This is hard . . .

Salesperson (playful tone) – Awesome! I love to help.

Distressed Salesperson

Using the Process Communication Model in sales enables salespeople to address the client according to that person's personality type and, if necessary, identify the client's distress signals to be able to neutralize them, as well as manage their own stress.

In a stress situation, the salesperson may develop negative behavior that can lead to failure. What are the reactions of a salesperson in distress?

When in distress, a salesperson with a **Thinker** personality type activates their Be Perfect for you driver. They feel obliged to be perfect, which means they tend to over-detail and over-inform. If this person meets a client with the same base, that person might think, "Here is someone who knows his job." However, if they are in negotiations with someone with a Harmonizer base, the client might feel, "This man is a real sourpuss. I doubt if I'll buy anything from him". The Rebel base client, "This guy is boring me to death. What is that thing? I don't get it." The client with a Promoter base, "If his product is as unexciting as he is, I don't need to buy it." The Imaginer type client risks feeling somewhat overwhelmed by all of the over-detail and wants much more summarized information.

The salesperson with a **Rebel** personality type who activates a Try Hard driver will have difficulty providing essential information in a simple, concise way. Most of the other personality types will perceive this person as unclear and the client will have trouble understanding the interest in the product.

A salesperson with a **Persister** type under the influence of the Be Perfect for me driver will tend to place him or herself in a dominant position, which will invite the client to feel inferior. The client may unwillingly buy out of submissiveness, or else rebel and think, "I don't want to buy anything from a guy like this. Who does he think he is?"

A salesperson with a **Harmonizer** base in distress will tend to want to please at all costs and over-adapt. They will "overdo it", causing the client to feel they are clingy or soft. They can also show difficulties in defining clear boundaries to an agreement or defending their own or their company's interests over those of the client. They can lose sight of their goals and get "bogged down" in the client relationship.

A salesperson with a **Promoter** type in distress showing the behavior of the Be Strong for me driver will make the client fend for themselves . . . .

In second degree distress, they can show a "high roller" side who is able to promise the moon. This type begins by creating a very positive atmosphere. They know how to be charming but if they "don't like" the person, they can be tempted to let the client figure out the product literature on her own. In a second phase, once the deal is made, they tend to drop the client, since follow-up holds no excitement. This is often frustrating for the client who could think, "I've been ripped off. He won't see me again."

A salesperson with an **Imaginer** type in distress will tend to not invest enough in the relationship. This will lead to negative consequences with clients for whom the quality of the relationship is an important source of motivation. In fact, few people with an Imaginer base are motivated by sales because it forces them to have frequent contact with the clientele.

At a time when sales is an increasingly demanding job, managing one's own stress is a significant advantage. The more a salesperson is aware of his or her own natural behavior, the more watchful they can become. For example, a **Thinker** type salesperson could be careful to avoid over-detailing and give only the information the client needs. The opposite would be the case for a **Promoter** type for whom giving information is not very exciting. This person might be inclined to say, "You'll find everything you need to know in the brochure," and should take care to support the client in discovering the product. For the **Rebel** type salesperson, the focus will be on providing information, taking a structured approach and not skipping any steps in the sales process. As for the **Persister** type, this profile can be careful to not come across as overly serious or a killjoy and should try to temper their "bulldozer" side. A salesperson with a **Harmonizer** type will need to learn to set positive boundaries without feeling uncomfortable so as not to be overrun by clients who are too demanding. The salesperson with an **Imaginer** base should take care to establish a "consistent" relationship with the client.

The salesperson's strengths, areas for vigilance and the sales process steps

Training a large number of salespeople in the Process Communication Model has helped us discover the strong points and points for improvement that are frequently found in each personality type. We have summarized these observations in Table 10.3. We have also observed a significant correlation between the steps in the sales process described by the salesperson as easy, and vice versa, the ones with which they have difficulties. Naturally, this table should be interpreted by taking the salesperson's personality structure into account, as well as the person's experience and what makes him or her unique.

A winning approach to sales

With training, salespeople can communicate with the client using the right communication channel, meeting the client's psychological need and using the client's preferred perception (table 10.4). To do so, they must begin by identifying the client's personality type and satisfying their own psychological needs, while remaining attentive to their own and their client's distress signals.

Table 10.3: Managing Stress to Improve Sales

Type	Strong points	Improvement points	Sales step +	Sales step -
Harmonizer	Quality contact Attentiveness Liste ning	Self-affirmation Ability to say no without discomfort	Contact	Conclusion (could settle for "spending a nice time with the client")
Thinker	Organization, method, meeting preparation, structuring	Flexibility Empathy	Knowledge Data gathering Summary	Contact (with the other personality types)
Persister	Rigor, method, reliability,	Casualness, playfulness, listening, analysis (tend to interpret)	Convincing	Contact (can seem too "parental" or moralizing)
Promoter	Adaptability, charm. Always has something to propose.	Empathy Support Follow-up	Contact Conclusion	Data gathering. Needs analysis (tend to use "readymade" solutions)
Rebel	Casualness, creativity	Rigor Organization	Contact Any solution requiring creativity.	Conclusion. (It can be laborious for this type.)
Imaginer	Listening, imagination, composure	Investment in the client relationship	Knowledge	Contact. Is not usually a "people person".

Table 10.4: The Winning Approach: Adapting to your Prospect

Type	Need	Perception	Channel
Harmonizer	Personal attention. "I'm interested in you as a person."	Emotion	Nurturative
Thinker	Recognition for their work. Structuring time. "I'll give you the facts and information you need and you decide."	Thought	Requestive
Persister	Respect for their convictions. Recognition for their work. "You can trust us, as well as our products and services."	Opinions	Requestive
Imaginer	Solitude. Directives. "Tell me what you want and I'll do the rest."	Inaction / imagination	Directive
Rebel	Playful Contact. "It's fun to work with you."	Reactions	Emotive
Promoter	Excitement. "I'm here to give you what you want for the best price."	Actions	Directive

CHAPTER 11

THE PROCESS COMMUNICATION MODEL
OR HOW TO SAY "I LOVE YOU"!

"All that brings people together is essential." Jean Moulin

Process Communication Model participants often begin experimenting with the model with their families. They "test" the channels and perceptions and explain the personality types and the dynamic of psychological needs to their spouse and children. This usually results in a wonderful moment of spontaneous meta-communication with very beneficial effects on the overall atmosphere.

Like anywhere else, miscommunication exists in marital life and in the parent-child relationship and can cause difficult family situations. "I don't understand my son or my wife."

Being able to interpret "problem behavior" and being able to decode its meaning helps reveal the appropriate response and avoid stress "overload". For example, considering one another's psychological needs facilitates the understanding and resolution of most conflicts between spouses; using the right communication channel and perception with one's child often enables considerable change in the relationship (while the more we insist on "pounding it into their head", the more stubborn they become). For a teacher, knowing that a student with a Rebel type does not learn the same way as one with a Thinker or Harmonizer base is very helpful in practicing individualized education.

MARITAL CONFLICT DYNAMICS

"When Mom and Dad fight, it's because they don't understand each other."

Matthew, age 8

In addition to a satisfying material and sexual life, the success of a couple largely depends on the spouse's satisfaction of his or her psychological needs. And, vice versa, the failure of a couple is often due to the fact that, little by little, the partners were unable to manage and maintain the relationship, allowing misunderstandings to accumulate until the pleasure and happiness definitively disappeared.

Different Perceptions

Eric and Marie took part in a couples' seminar to try to resolve a serious crisis. Before the seminar, Eric was considering leaving Marie. He is 28 years old and has an Imaginer base and a Rebel phase. He is a special-needs teacher specializing in prevention. All day long, he is in contact with needy teens.

> When I come home at night, I'm tired. I want quiet. I want to stretch out on the couch, listen to music, read a good book or just do nothing. Marie has a lot of difficulty with my attitude. She feels left out. She complains and tells me that if I loved her I would take her in my arms and be close to her. I feel invaded by her demands and I crawl into my shell and withdraw psychologically. I sometimes even go out to get some air.

What is happening here? Eric gets his Rebel phase psychological needs met all day long. In the evening, he needs solitude, which indicates that he "goes back down" to his Imaginer base.

Marie has a Harmonizer base and phase. She is very much in love with Eric and expects the same feelings in return. In the evening, she is very demanding for warmth and tenderness. She interprets Eric's cold, distant behavior as a sign of detachment and loss of interest.

Due to this, despite the love they feel for each other, each partner invites the other into distress. The more "absent" Eric is, the more Marie demands love and the more Marie demands love, the more Eric withdraws. Each one is naturally convinced that the other is the origin of the problem: if Eric were more attentive, Marie would feel better. And for Eric, if Marie were less intrusive, he could breathe better.

Once they realize the real meaning of the problem, Marie and Eric can find more appropriate answers to their mutual needs.

Eric – I realize that Marie isn't trying to "eat me alive" or be intrusive. She has a Harmonizer base and phase and needs warmth and tenderness.

Marie – I thought I wasn't important to Eric anymore. Now I understand that since he has an Imaginer base, he first needs quiet and solitude at the end of the day when he has been "frazzled" by his job.

Many marital conflicts can be avoided and replaced by more rewarding intimacy if the partners understand each other's inner life and learn to talk about their relationship. Plus, when each one accepts their share of responsibility in the conflict, it becomes much easier to resolve the problem.

Many sources of misunderstanding in a couple come from the fact that each person expects the other to perceive life the same way.

- "It's normal to think before acting," states the Thinker type.
- "Anyone who is not in contact with their feelings is emotionally disabled," says the Harmonizer type.
- "What matters most in a person are their values and opinions," believes the Persister type.
- "The only thing that pays off is action," cries the Promoter type.
- "For me it's simple: I like it or I dislike it," the Rebel type reacts.
- "What's important is our inner life," murmurs the Imaginer type.

Patrick and Jenny's story illustrates the difficulties many couples encounter in understanding and accepting the other's difference.

Patrick and Jenny are a "happy couple", married for about ten years. Patrick is a senior executive in the food industry. Jenny works part-time in the social sector and devotes the rest of her time to her children.

Patrick has a Thinker base and phase, Jenny a Harmonizer base and phase.

One night, Patrick came home at 8 p.m. as usual. He saw that his wife was upset and asked her what's wrong.

- "I don't know, I'm just upset," she answers in a tired, plaintive voice.
- "I can see that you're upset, but what's going on?" he asks again, this time with slight impatience in his tone.
- "I just don't know," I said. "I'm upset that's all." Jenny is about to cry.
- "No," he snaps, "you're not going to do that again. I asked you to explain, that's all."
- "You don't understand me, you just don't understand me," repeats Jenny who starts to cry.

Patrick is frustrated. It is true that he doesn't understand and that he hates to not understand. He leaves the room slamming the door and remembers the old belief that women are just incapable of explaining themselves without drama.

Jenny, who felt bad before her husband came home, now feels terrible, misunderstood and unloved.

Let's observe what happened. Jenny is in distress and overwhelmed by emotion. She cannot immediately access her thinking part and give her husband the information he asks for. Patrick needs information to be able to think about how to solve the problem. Since he is frustrated in his need, he also becomes distressed and cannot access his Harmonizer part. Jenny tries to communicate with her husband through emotions while Patrick needs to exchange via thought. In other words, each person unconsciously tries to impose their own frame of reference on the other. This creates and then reinforces the distress in each of them, covering up the problem and inhibiting their ability to resolve it.

The couple will be able to reestablish communication and come out of distress by understanding each other's dynamics. For example, Patrick can agree to be warm and comforting even if he does not understand and Jenny can learn to manage her emotions and not interpret misunderstanding as a sign of not being loved.

Phase Changes

Phase changes in one or both partners often leads to a period of more or less severe turbulence in a couple. The couple enters a period of incommunicability; what used to create the union's solidity now seems unattainable or outdated.

Let's take two examples of phase changes:

David married Jo-Anne 17 years ago. They have three children who are growing up without any particular problems. David has a Persister base and phase and Jo-Ann a Harmonizer base and phase. David recalls that he first liked Jo-Ann for her compassion. She dreamed of having children and raising them together.

They were very happy together for many years. They tacitly divided their roles. Jo-Ann took care of the house and children. She made sure that it was a pleasant home, enjoyed receiving their many friends and she maintained good relations with their respective families. David attached a lot of importance to transmitting values to his children. His job absorbed most of his time but he tried to be available to his wife and children on the weekend. He was the one who made the decisions on investments, the children's schooling and their vacations.

His wife's behavior changed. She asked about going back to work. When her husband refused on the grounds of the children's education, she demanded a role change and asked David to help more with the household chores. David did not take to this well. Tension rose and, naturally, the more Jo-Ann demanded, the more stubborn David became and the more stubborn David became the more Jo-Ann demanded.

How can we analyze this crisis that David & Jo-Ann just experienced? David married a women with a Harmonizer base and phase and he expected her to function in Harmonizer. Their couple had worked very well until then because their respective needs were satisfied. He had a life that fit his values; she was the nourishing mother and felt happy with her life.

Then Jo-Ann "phased" into Thinker. Her motivations and behavior changed. Her role as exclusively a good wife and mother no longer met her aspirations. She sought a new kind of fulfillment. David was destabilized by this new behavior (people with a Persister base often do not like change and seek continuity). He no longer recognizes the woman he loves and does not like who she has become.

Let's take another example:

Frank is 41 years old, a senior executive in the aeronautics industry. At the age of 26, he married Janine and they have a 14 year-old daughter. Frank has a Thinker base and phase. What he liked about Janine, who has an Imaginer base and phase, was her quiet, serious side. He always felt more peaceful when he was with her. He particularly liked her independence and the long discussions they had together. He easily told friends that his wife was independent. Once in a while, he confided stories about his childhood and described a very intrusive, over-bearing mother. "With Janine, at least I can breathe."

Recently Frank has a new feeling that he doesn't like. (It is not infrequent for people with a Thinker base to feel uncomfortable with, as they say, "irrational" thoughts). What he feels is boredom. Long discussions no longer interest him, the calm and quiet in his life have become suffocating (and he hates to recall that childhood feeling). In other words, as he puts it, he feels like "raising hell". In reaction to her husband's attempts to get her to change her behavior, Janine tends to keep quiet and crawl into her shell, which invites Frank to be angry. For a long time he had wanted to buy a motorcycle, let his hair grow out and buy a leather jacket. Now he likes brightly colored shirts and sometimes even goes to the office in jeans. Of course, he starts having trouble with his manager. He tends to complain about how monotonous his job is and starts to look for a job where he can use his creativity more. In other words, Frank has gone into Rebel phase and is "suffocating" in what he now sees as a "Thinker straight jacket". While his private and business life once satisfied him completely, he now feels out of sync.

Many divorces can be analyzed in terms of one of the partners phasing. In the two examples above, the psychological "work" to be done for David is to accept Jo-Ann's "natural" change because if the psychological needs of her phase are not satisfied, she will be frustrated, which will have repercussions on the couple and family. Accepting change in the other and establishing a new balance often requires appropriate support. The couple can have friends who support them through the crisis or they may seek help from specialists.

The Frank-Janine couple will probably suffer a severe crisis. It often occurs that people with a Thinker base who phase into Rebel display "perfect Rebel" behavior and their loved ones are surprised. "He's going through adolescent crisis at his age!" It is not unusual for them to completely question their private and business life.

Bruno is 40 years old and is "fed up" with his life. He managed to get himself fired. With his severance package, he treated himself to 2 ½ years of traveling the world. He asked for a divorce and remarried a young 26 year-old Tahitian. Now he has a regular job again and just one dream: having enough money to retire at 50.

CONFLICT WITH CHILDREN

Problems in the parent-child relationship often appear when one of the parents who has a different base or phase does not understand the child's needs or mode of functioning. Here is an example.

> Steve is a sixteen year-old high-school student. His father, who has a Persister base in Thinker phase, feels that his career is a failure. He expects a lot from his only son. Steve is an all-A student with a Thinker base. He perfectly meets his father's desire for him to become a doctor and allows his Dad to exert strict control over his studies. When he became a senior, he "all of a sudden" phased into his Rebel floor. Now he wants more and more to do as he pleases, which his father does not accept. "Attend to your schoolwork first, then you'll do what you want." Little by little, tension develops in the relationship. The father becomes more and more rigid, the son more and more negative Rebel. Steve displays very provocative behavior, contesting parental authority and compromising his future education.

But don't all teens go through a "Rebel phase"? Although most go through a more or less durable period of rebellion, it is not because of a PCM phase change. Teen rebellion is usually a reaction to a system the teen sees – rightly so, or not – as "negative Persister", which invites rebellious reactions. This is also the period during which invitations to distress and miscommunication are most frequent.

Parents who realize there is some kind of blockage in their relationship with their children are often surprised to see how much the situation improves when they change their mode of communication.

Their biggest difficulty is the fact of the extreme speed of the change in their offspring, the constant bubbling cauldron, the mood swings, and the often "volcanic" behavior that goes with them. For most parents, this period is a source of distress because they must deal with the teen's demands for independence. As the youngster strives to break ties and pushes the limits to see how far he can go, parents worry about the child's schooling, health, drug abuse, etc. This is when parent-child communication is probably most important but also the most difficult. A philosophy teacher told us that in senior year, 8 out of 10 teens say they can't talk to their parents about things they really care about.

INDIVIDUALIZING CHILD-REARING

Just like managers, parents sometimes hesitate to individualize their mode of communication. Let's take the case of a family with one child who has a Thinker base and another child with a Rebel base. The first child was able to do his homework on his own at a very young age. He is organized and has no problem getting down to work. His brother with a Rebel base does not have the same motivation at all. If his parents expect the same of him, they are headed towards conflict. Let's imagine a child with a Rebel base whom we ask to help with a chore like setting the table. We usually get a series of sighs and hmmff's and very clear resistance. Let's imagine a parent with a Persister base who states, "It's only normal, you need to learn responsibility. And you can stop complaining," which will only worsens the problem. On the other hand, if the parent takes a playful approach and says something like, "Try to complain as loudly as you can while you set the table," it is more likely to lead to positive results and setting the table becomes... child's play!

The "parent-child couples" most likely to encounter difficulties:

- The Rebel base teen hates to be hugged and cuddled if he or she not in the mood. The mother with a Harmonizer base can feel unloved by her child and use "emotional blackmail".
- While the Dad with a Persister type could try to convince the teen. "Son, that's just how it is. I wasn't allowed to answer my father back."
- With a Persister base child, that same dad could also encounter difficulties, with each one preaching their beliefs without

listening to the other. During a supervision group, one of the trainees with a Persister base told us the following:

> I use the Process Communication Model with my son a lot. He is three years-old and already acts like an affirmed Persister type! When he's got an idea in his head he sticks to it and won't give up. I have to be careful to keep my calm. When he talks to me, it's with, "I'm right, Dad, aren't I?" "You're not allowed to do that!" "I'm allowed to." "I can." "I want." I don't mean to caricaturize, he does "travel through his floors" like everyone else, but in a situation of tension, all the signs are there.

The father with the Promoter base risks losing interest in a son with a Harmonizer base who perceives the world not through action but though emotions and sensations.

To each our own style.

Some parents believe it is fundamental to show a united front to the children and not express any disagreement in their child-rearing choices, even if it means conflict. Unfortunately, this overlooks the fact that the way they understand their child's behavior depends on their own personality types. And for this reason, it is subject to diverging natural perceptions. Here is an illustration:

> Situation: A child comes home from school with detention for disrupting the class.
>
> Parental reactions:
>
> Persister – It's important for you to have the image of a responsible person. You're also grounded on Saturday night.
>
> Thinker – How are you going to fill your time during detention?
>
> Harmonizer – My poor darling, you must've been put up to it.

Rebel – Detention is the most fun thing about school!

Promoter – You see, what's important is not getting caught.

Imaginer – Oh so, you won't be home tomorrow after school.

While we're on the subject, we should point out that schoolwork is a perfect place to experiment with the Process Communication Model. The better a parent understands a child's behavior, the better they know the keys to their motivation. There is no point in letting a child with a Rebel or Promoter type sit and be bored for two hours behind an empty desk. It is better to send him out to play some hoops or any other game that energizes him. Afterwards, there is a high chance that the child will have the energy to climb to his or her Thinker floor. Firmly sending a Harmonizer type child off to do their homework without showing support will probably cause the child to make "stupid" mistakes. Assuring him that we love him for himself and feel close to him contributes more to this child's scholastic success. Forcing an Imaginer base to play on a football team or head a boy-scout troop is the best way to put him in distress. And "silencing" a Thinker-Persister by telling him "he just doesn't understand," is the surest way to weaken his self-confidence.

AT SCHOOL

Many parents will find this familiar. All of a sudden, their child who had always been very good at math, seems to have lost her intelligence. When they ask the child why her grades have gone down, she usually blames the teacher. "I don't understand anything with him." "If I ask a question, he shuts me up."

In teaching, as elsewhere, student performance largely depends on the quality of the relationship the child has with the teacher. Are they in sync or not? Who hasn't heard, "History and geography have always bored me, all through school, except one year when the teacher was so great, so lively, that we drank in his words."

We conducted a study on a population of 300 students who were considered "at risk". This meant that their negative behavior was so severe and so frequent that they risked compromising their studies.

This research showed[31] that 295 of them had the Thinker phase on the last floor of their condominium and for the most part had a Rebel or Promoter base. We can easily imagine the energy they must have had to invest in a system designed by (and for) teachers with Persister or Thinker personality types. Wouldn't the ideal teacher for these students be someone like the literature teacher in Dead Poets Society, a "wonderful" Persister in Rebel phase who wants to get his message across and does so playfully?

In the learning process, the most effective teaching method is the one that addresses:

- Emotions for the Harmonizer type students: it is fundamental for them to feel close to their teacher. They will want to perform well and will make the effort to learn in order to please the teacher and parents;
- Facts and structured time for the Thinker type students who usually do not encounter too many difficulties at school;
- Also facts for the young Persister and Imaginer types who function well in an informative system. Students with a Persister base like to see things through to the end. While the young Imaginer base student will sometimes experience distress during timed exams out of fear of not being able to finish on time.
- Play and experimentation for the Rebel type;
- Excitement and a high energy level for the Promoter type students (a difficult challenge, admittedly). They often give their best in sports.

A seminar participant who runs a technical school explained how she uses the Process Communication Model in her job.

> In our schools, it's always about "you must do this." But our students are learning a manual trade because, at some point, they failed and it was always due to emotional reasons. At some point they did not receive the recognition they needed. That is why it is important to use the right communication channel to address each person's reality. It also helps me to guide them in their relationships with their teachers. It helps

---

[31] Interview between Gérard Collignon and Taibi Kahler in Little Rock, July 1990.

them to understand that they have the right to be angry and to criticize but that they have every interest in expressing it in a way that gets the message across.

And does it work?

Yes. In any case, it works for me! In difficult situations, I can have a dialogue in which I don't get irritated or feel like I would be more effective if I just preached at them. I even say to some of them, "I took a seminar called the Process Communication Model. You realize that…, etc." They are happy because we are on equal footing. I am also in a learning situation.

A chapter written by Jérôme Lefeuvre, Certifying Master Trainer, Process Communication Model®.

Modern and ancient heroes in the eye of PCM.

Enhancing the quality of life and relationships has been the motto of Kahler Communications, Inc. for many years.

PCM offers keys and tools for a better life. And each of us is and has been looking for clues and models to make it happen.

Taibi Kahler, after Berne reflected on a wonderful metaphor for our failure patterns in Greek mythology, contemplating cursed heroes bearing the burden of a doomed life wondered how close they were from us. And he made a fascinating connection between Hercules, Arachne, Cassandra, Sisyphus, Damocles and Tantalus with recurring failure patterns in Phase of personality.

How many more Greek mythology heroes would be recognizable through PCM lenses? Probably most if not all of them.

Look at Ulysses (Homer's not Joyce's). He was cursed by Poseidon for having blinded and then killed his cyclops son, Polyphemus. The worst agony Poseidon found to punish Ulysses was to make sure he would forget his goal and seduce him into delaying it forever. Ulysses goal? Well he just wanted to go back to his home town and his wife Penelope. His one and only true love.

Unlike Achilles or Hector, Ulysses, a real down to earth kind of guy, did not crave power and glory. He dreamt of fresh bread, wine from his vine and the warmth of his wife's arms.

Ten years fighting the idiotic Trojan wars (which he won alone with his cunning horse by the way) and then ten more years to get back home, while rejecting the love of the magnificent witch Circe, or the seductive Calypso and insensitive to the sirens' songs... he eventually finds his way back home.

There you are. Here is our typical Promoter bonding issue: *always* trapped failure pattern, manipulative at times, cunning and determined at other times. The point being here that anyone who wishes to learn form the ancient what lies within the Promoter Personality Type will find it in Homer's Iliad's hero Ulysses.

And today, where are the doomed heroes? Have you been going to the movies the past fifteen years? Did you see the rise of the superheroes? Here they are again, names have been changed and still we write, play and make movies about them.

Is it that new? Well let's go back another twenty years. Star Trek and Mr. Spock or Captain James T. Kirk are so very archetypal aren't they?

"Captain on the Bridge"

Star Trek, great PCM types:

The TV show Star Trek in the 60's became a cult series. Daring and profoundly humanist the show portrayed a crew of high rank officers including a black woman, a Russian, and an Asian man sharing the deck of a starship. Most of this had never been seen on TV before.

The writers of the show imagined a race of logical beings who had evolved past the need for emotion, living on planet Vulcan, whose main perception of life and events was factual thoughts on measurable information. Mr Spock, son of a Vulcan dad and a human mom and probably the most popular character on the show, made the Thinker Type a star in itself. Viewers and fans would wait passionately for his rational reactions facing danger, love, or humor.

Still, rumor has it that he changed Phase and even worse, his Base might not be what we all thought.

If we agree a Vulcan Base is Thinker, the following dialogue with this father, Sarek, about his human mother's murder comes as a surprise:

Spock: I am as conflicted as I once was as a child.
Sarek: You will always be a child of two worlds. I am grateful for this... and for you.
Spock: I feel anger for the one who took Mother's life - an anger I *cannot* control.
Sarek: I believe... that she would say, "Do not try to." You asked me once why I married your mother. I married her because I loved her.

Do Vulcans phase just like us? Seems so. Sarek speaks a language of emotion and his gratefulness for an uncontrollable phenomenon does not sound so logical after all. In the movie *Into Darkness* the script writers took things even further implying that as a boy Spock Base was not Thinker but Persister. Reaching the age of adulthood he has to decide whether he is ready to become a mature Vulcan and join the Vulcan academy. With his results on the exam being perfect he faces the council who says something shocking to him. Instead of embarking into a crusade against the system, he decides to change his life and observe things rationally. He might be showing here that his Base might be Persister and Thinker a cultural and educational resource.

Vulcan Council President: You have surpassed the expectations of your instructors. Your final record is flawless, with one exception: I see that you have applied to Starfleet as well.
Spock: It was logical to cultivate multiple options.
Vulcan Council President: Logical but unnecessary. You are hereby accepted to the Vulcan Science Academy. It is truly remarkable, Spock, that you have achieved so much despite your disadvantage. All rise.
[*the Vulcan Council stands in honor of Spock who now looks slightly pissed*]
Spock: If you would clarify, Minister: to what disadvantage are you referring?
Vulcan Council President: Your human mother.
Spock: Council... Ministers, I must decline.
Vulcan Council President: No Vulcan has ever declined admission to this academy!
Spock: Then, as I am half-human, your record remains untarnished.

Sarek: Spock, you have made a commitment to honor the Vulcan way.

Vulcan Council President: Why did you come before this council today? Was it to satisfy your emotional need to rebel?

Spock: The only emotion I wish to convey is gratitude. Thank you, Ministers, for your consideration.

[*In a tone reserved for preaching*]

Spock: Live long and prosper.

This might come as a mind blowing revelation to fans but it seems that Vulcans were not born thinkers and instead seem to make it a personal growth process. Ah! Of course the matter is open for debate.

Captain Kirk is a simpler character altogether. Cunning and charming he built a team of all types of personality (and interstellar races) to make sure he could *go boldly were no other man has ever gone before* on his ship "Enterprise" with the best crew from all worlds of the entire universe. I rest my case here.

The Hulk and Frankenstein creature, Harmonizers in distress

Bruce Banner was a young Base Thinker scientist who phased into Harmonizer when he experienced the loss of his humanity. Poisoned by radiation he now has to suffer the emotional issue of anger in his new Phase. He will have to hide in order to protect the woman he loves because he cannot control his anger. When this happens he turns into a super strong green monster who will hit and destroy anything around him. There he is now making sure he never gets angry since he knows if he does he might make some stupid unforgivable mistakes.

In 1933, James Whale gave life in a beautiful and heart-breaking flick to Dr. Frankenbstein's creature, as played by Boris Karloff. This poor lost soul wants nothing but a friend who will love him. He is so clumsy and ugly looking that his desperate attempts to connect end up in screams or accidental killings on his part. It appears to the PCM expert he came (back) to life with a Base/Phase Harmonizer. Ill-equipped Channel and Perception wise, his nurturative communication remains misunderstood by all except the blind man who lives in the forest. As he spends some time with him, we find clearly what his needs are when he learns to speak and his first words are: *Wine good, friend good, fire bad.*

Sensory needs and recognition as a person would have helped. Yet his appearance led him to the conclusion that he was not loveable, his existential question. Unable to contain his anger, the script writers did not offer us a Phase change and we may ask how the story would have ended if he had been loved and cherished. In Mary Shelley's book, he chooses to leave western civilization and lose himself in the North Pole silence. Two possible interpretations: he Phased Imaginer or he went down third degree distress and died in the cold.

A recent TV show titled *"Penny Dreadful"* (spoiler alert)........................... decided to explore another possibility. The Frankenstein creature turns out to be a very sensitive human being, poetry lover, who is compassionate, gentle and warm. He has to fight his way back into humanity through love after having dealt with his issue of anger. This show decided to allow the character to find peace through the meeting of needs, dealing with the issue and the existential question when his family accepts him back the way he looks and gives nothing but unconditional love to him.

The fight between Persister Base and Persister Phase, Captain America and Iron Man

In the 2016, epic adventure of the Avengers, *"Civil War"* a very interesting and logical issue was raised which was a relief for all Thinker Base viewers in the world. Every time the superheroes came in to fight evil, they destroyed half of the city they were supposed to protect. There had to be casualties if one looked at it rationally. Until today no one seemed to even raise an eyebrow about this.

In the previous episode of the saga we had witnessed Iron Man Phase from Promoter to Persister. No more showing off, no more seducing everyone. His new need: uphold the law and bring some meaning to the Avengers mission.

(Spoiler alert) ....
....

In this episode, the government, tired of cleaning the mess left by them, demands to the Avengers to become agents of the State and go and fight only when told to do so.

Iron Man takes the lead, as a Promoter and Persister, who else? Nobody knows where Hulk is, apart from you, dear reader, you know he is dealing with his issue of anger somewhere else safe.

Captain American, noble Persister Base and Phase first agrees to the new terms and finds himself in a bind when he decides to break his vow to defend an old friend.

The damages of the fight between the two Persister oriented friends is tremendous. I remember, as a viewer, thinking: "Wow this is not a fun show anymore. There are some serious issues here. Nevertheless, enjoyable, even though two crusades facing one another is a scary thing to watch.

We could go on and on identifying super Heroes connections with PCM. I leave you the pleasure of reflecting on Spiderman Rebel issues, or Batman cunning overcontroling martyr of the cause complex personality Phase changes.

Enjoy! PCM offers endless fun analysis in traditional and pop culture.

CONCLUSION

Our trainees often tell us, "PCM saved my family's life", "PCM saved my relationship." The Process Communication Model® does not have the power to save. Yet it is a powerful tool when we know how to use it. "Oh, if only I'd known PCM 10 years ago, I wouldn't have made the same mistakes," is also something we hear quite often. Or, "Now I know I'm not crazy. I just have an atypical profile." I hope that you have also found answers to your questions on behavior management after reading this wonderful book.

For some of us, beginning with the author, the Process Communication Model® is much more than a tool. It's a way of life. That is why Gérard and I have the ambition to spread the word to the masses, all around the world. It is our daily privilege to be supported by our partners/distributors, Master Trainers, trainers and coaches who are talented professionals with a passion for this model. We are assisted by our highly-qualified teams who make this ambition a reality.

Kahler Communication's mission is to help improve the quality of each person's life by helping us understand one another better and communicate better. Our aim is to improve self-knowledge in order to feel better, improve our knowledge of others in order to better understand our differences, and lastly and most difficult, to better manage our relationships.

Dr. Taibi Kahler regularly tells us that we are in authentic +/+ only 5 to 10% of the time. Fortunately, we are not in second degree distress. Unless we undergo intense training, our express drivers and message become unclear. Humans focus on the content when they speak, however the form is more important. How then do we handle the heavy task of managing a loved one who shows a second degree distress mask? It is highly probable that reading this book is only a first step in communicating differently next time.

Managing relationships is a complex and universal process. That is why we have established Process Communication Model® seminars all around the world with numerous applications like Management & Leadership, Team Effectiveness, Coaching, Sales, Human Resources, Education, and Family. We offer seminars on several levels: 1-Initiation, 2-Practice, 3-Expert. These seminars are systematically run by a certified trainer. The coaching sessions are offered by a coach who is certified in this model. We have 2,500 certified trainers today around the world and our goal is to heavily develop this worldwide network to make it reflect the power of the Process Communication Model®. We hope this book has contributed to this goal in its own way.

Cyril Collignon, President, Kahler Communications, Inc.

To Know More

Contact Kahler Communications, Inc.

Kahler Communications, Inc.
P.O. Box 23230
Hot Springs, AR 71903-3230 USA
+1-501-276-0688
www.kahlercomcommunications.com

KAHLER COMMUNICATIONS, INC. COPYRIGHTED ELEMENTS

[Printed for legal reasons]

1. The six Personality Types: Workaholic (now called Thinker), Reactor (now called Harmonizer), Persister, Dreamer (now called Imaginer), Rebel, Promoter. Taibi Kahler, Ph.D., *Director*, Kahler Communications, Inc., Little Rock, Arkansas, 1988, 1992, 2000, 2004.

2. The personality structure is made up of the six Personality Types.

The personality building Taibi Kahler, Ph.D. *Process Communication Management Seminar*, Taibi Kahler Associates, Inc., Little Rock, Arkansas, October 1982, 1996.

3. Each Personality Type shows three character strengths: Workaholic (responsible, logical, organized); Harmonizer (compassionate, sensitive, warm); Persister (observant, dedicated, conscientious); Dreamer (imaginative, reflective, calm); Rebel (spontaneous, creative, playful); Promoter (adaptable, charming, resourceful). Taibi Kahler, Ph.D., *Manager*, Kahler Communications, Inc., Little Rock, Arkansas, 1988, 1992, 2000, 2004

4. These six Personality Types are found in each of us with a different sequence of strengths from the age of seven, and generally don't change. Stansbury, Pat, *Report of Adherence,* according to the observations on the same subject with the help of the Personal Pattern Inventory that was taken twice. Kahler Communications, Inc., Little Rock, Arkansas, 1990.

5. Each Personality Type has his/her own personal management and relationship style; the Workaholic and Persister use the democratic style, the Reactor uses the democratic style, the Rebel uses the laissez-faire style, the Promoter uses and Dreamer accepts the autocratic style. Taibi Kahler, Ph.D.,

Manager, Kahler Communications, Inc., Little Rock, Arkansas, 1988, 1992, 2000, 2004.

6. The identified personality parts are: protector, sensor, comforter, director, computer, and emoter. Taibi Kahler, Ph.D. *Process Communication Management Seminar*, Taibi Kahler Associates, Inc., Little Rock, Arkansas, October 1982, 1996

7. Each Personality Type has a corresponding personality part: Workaholic, Persister and Dreamer use the computer part; Reactor uses the comforter part; the Rebel uses the emoter part; the Promoter uses the director. Taibi Kahler, Ph.D., *Process Communication Management Seminar*, Taibi Kahler Associates, Inc., Little Rock, Arkansas, October 1982, 1996.

8. Five channels are identified: interventive channel (1) makes the offer from the protector and is accepted by the sensor; directive channel (2) makes the offer from the director and is accepted by the computer; the requestive channel (3) makes the offer from the computer and is accepted by the computer; the nurturative channel (4) makes the offer from the comforter and is accepted by the emoter; the emotive channel (5) makes an offer from the emoter and is accepted by the emoter.

Taibi Kahler, Ph.D., *Process Communication Management Seminar*, Taibi Kahler Associates, Inc., Little Rock, Arkansas, October 1982, 1996.

9. Persister and Workaholic types use the requestive channel (3) together. Promoter transmits on the directive channel (2) towards the Dreamer; the Rebel uses the emotive channel (5) together; the Harmonizer uses the nurturative channel together and towards the rebel.

Taibi Kahler, Ph. D., *Process Communication Management Seminar*, Taibi Kahler Associates, Inc., Little Rock, Arkansas, October 1982, 1996.

10. The following perceptions correspond to the listed personality types:

1   Workaholic: thoughts
2   Persister: opinions
3   Harmonizer: emotions
4   Dreamer: inaction
5   Rebel: reactions (I like..," "I don't like...")
6   Promoter: actions

Taibi Kahler, Ph.D., *Manager*, Kahler Communications, Inc., Little Rock, Arkansas, 1988, 1992, 2000, 2004.

11. Each Personality Type has a preferential environment, according to the following matrix: the vertical line is the goal axis; the horizontal is the relationship axis. The upper point is called internal motivation; the lower point is called external motivation. The point on the left is called engaged; the point on the right is called in retreat.

This forms the four quadrants. The upper left quadrant contains the Reactor type that prefers groups, the upper right quadrant contains the Persister and Workaholic types that prefer one-to-one relationships, the lower right quadrant contains the dreamer type that prefers to be alone, the lower left quadrant contains the rebel and promoter types that prefer to go from group to group or be on the edges of varied groups.

Taibi Kahler, Ph.D. *Process Communication Management Seminar*, Taibi Kahler Associates, Inc., Little Rock, Arkansas, October 1982, 1996.

12. Each Personality Type has received a recurrent theme (AKA "the existentialist question"):

7 Workaholic: "Am I competent?"
8 Persister: "Am I worthy of confidence?"
9 Promoter: "Am I alive?"
10 Dreamer: "Am I wanted?"
11 Rebel: "Am I acceptable?"
12 Harmonizer: "Am I likeable?"

Spencer/Shenk/Capers and Taibi Kahler Associates. *Process Communication Seminar*, Gardena, California, 1989 ; Taibi Kahler, Ph.D., Building Quality Teams, Kahler Communications, Inc., Little Rock, Arkansas. 1990, 1996.

13. Personality type phases and psychological needs:

13 Workaholic [phase]: needs recognition for work and structured time.
14 Persister [phase]: needs recognition for work and convictions.
15 Harmonizer [phase]: needs recognition of person, sensory satisfaction.
16 Rebel [phase]: needs contact.
17 Dreamer [phase]: needs solitude.
18 Promoter [phase]: needs excitement.

Taibi Kahler, Ph.D., *Manager*, Kahler Communication, Inc., Little Rock, Arkansas, 1988, 1992, 2000, 2004.

14. Three degrees of stress: First degree-the entry door; second degree-the basement; third degree-the cellar. Taibi Kahler, Ph.D. *Process Communication Management Seminar*, Taibi Kahler Associates, Inc., Little Rock, Arkansas, October 1982, 1996

15. Drivers are: "the observable behavior of negative miniscript sequences." Taibi Kahler discovered the five base *drivers*: "Please others," "Try hard," "Be perfect," "Be strong," "Hurry up," with which there are corresponding words, tone of voice, gestures, postures, and facial expressions. Taibi Kahler, Ph.D., with Hedges Capers, Div. M, LHD. "The Miniscript," *Transactional Analysis Journal*, 4:1, pp. 26-42, January 1974.

16. Each personality type has a primary *driver*: workaholic - be perfect (I have to be perfect for others); persister - be perfect (for me); harmonizer - please others; rebel - try hard (I must try hard for others); dreamer - be strong (I must be strong for others); promoter - be strong (for me). Taibi Kahler, Ph.D. *Process Communication Management Seminar*, Taibi Kahler Associates, Inc., Little Rock, Arkansas, October 1982, 1996.

17. A first degree of "mismanagement" behavior is associated with each type of personality *driver*:

> Workaholic -"Be perfect": the manager does not delegate well;

> Persister - "Be perfect" (for me): the manger focuses on what is not going well and is not good;

> Harmonizer - "Please others": the manager is too attached to the well being of others and has problems taking decisions;

> Rebel - "Try hard (I must try hard for others)": the manager has problems knowing what to do and delegates badly:

> Dreamer - "Be strong (I must be strong for others)"; the manager waits for things to take care of themselves and does not take decisions;

> Promoter - "Be strong (for me)": does not provide support ("figure it out for yourself").

Taibi Kahler, Ph.D., *Manager*, Kahler Communication, Inc., Little Rock, Arkansas, 1988, 1992, 2000, 2004.

18. At the second degree of stress each Personality Type displays a failure mechanism: the Workaholic over controls; the Persister imposes personal beliefs; the Reactor makes mistakes; the Rebel blames; the Dreamer waits passively; the Promoter manipulates. Taibi Kahler, Ph.D., *Manager*, Kahler Communication, Inc., Little Rock, Arkansas, 1988, 1992, 2000, 2004.

19. At the second degree of stress each Personality Type wears a mask: the Workaholic and the Persister wear an attacker's mask; the Harmonizer and the Dreamer wear the mask of a victim; the Rebel and the Promoter wear the mask of a blamer. The masks are identifiable with words, tone of voice, gestures, postures, and facial expressions.

Taibi Kahler, Ph.D. *Process Communication Management Seminar*, Taibi Kahler Associates, Inc., Little Rock, Arkansas, October 1982, 1996.

20. At the second degree of stress each personality type displays warning signals:

1   Workaholic: frustrated when others don't think logically, gets obsessed with time, money, order, cleanliness;
2   Persister: extremely sensitive to criticism, becomes suspicious and critical. Believes that only his/her opinions are right;
3   Harmonizer: no longer confident, laughs at him/herself inappropriately, invites criticism;
4   Rebel: appears negative, complains. Uses "yes but" with others, and blames others, events and situations;
5   Dreamer: withdraws into passiveness, no initiative, and projects are not finished;
6   Promoter: starts fights, ignores or breaks rules, and manipulates others.

Taibi Kahler, Ph.D. *Process Communication Management Seminar*, Taibi Kahler Associates, Inc., Little Rock, Arkansas, October 1982, 1996.

21. At the second degree of stress each personality type displays life position behavior:

7   Workaholic and Persister display; "I'm OK / You're not OK";
8   Harmonizer and Dreamer display: "I'm not OK / You're OK";

9   Rebel and Promoter display: "I'm OK / You're not OK."

Taibi Kahler, Ph.D. *Process Communication Management Seminar*, Taibi Kahler Associates, Inc., Little Rock, Arkansas, October 1982, 1996.

22. At the third degree of stress each personality type foresees a negative final benefit:

10 Workaholic: wants to exclude those that do not think clearly;

11 Persister: wants to exclude those that are not reliable;

12 Harmonizer: feels he/she will be excluded because "they no longer love me";

13 Dreamer: waits to be told what to do and is surprised when excluded;

14 Promoter: wants to exclude those that can't take it.

15 When an individual displays a *driver,* the appropriate intervention model is the use of the channel and perception associated with the type revealed by the *driver.*

16 with "Be perfect (for you)" use the requestive channel and thought;

17 with "Be perfect (for me)", use the requestive channel and opinions;

18 with "Please others (for you)" use the nurturative channel and emotions;

19 with "Try hard (for you)" use the emotive channel and reactions [I like/I don't like];

20 with "Be strong (for you)" use the directive channel and inaction;

21 with "Be strong (for me)" use the directive channel and actions

Taibi Kahler, Ph.D., *The Advanced PCM Seminar*, Kahler Communications, Inc., Little Rock, Arkansas, 1997.

24. Each phase type of the Personality Type has potential problematics which determine whether an individual will or will not change phase in the course of a lifetime:

22 Workaholic: sorrow linked to loss;

23 Persister: fear;

24 Harmonizer: anger;

25 Rebel: responsibility;

26 Dreamer: autonomy;

27 Promoter: contacts.

Taibi Kahler, Ph.D., *The Advanced PCM Seminar*, Kahler Communications, Inc., Little Rock, Arkansas, 1997.

25. Each base Personality Type has a script with a failure sequence that is observable in speech patterns:
Workaholic and Persister: "Until";

28 Harmonizer: "After";
29 Rebel and Promoter: "Always";
30 Dreamer: "Never."

Certain combinations of Personality Types produce the scripts "Almost 1" and "Almost 2" Professional and Personal.

Taibi Kahler, Ph.D., *Process Communication Management Seminar*, Taibi Kahler Associates, Inc., Little Rock, Arkansas, October 1982 ; Taibi Kahler, Ph.D., *The Advanced PCM Seminar*, Kahler Communications, Inc., Little Rock, Arkansas, 1997.

26. The four myths are: "I have the power to make you feel good"; "I have the power to make you feel bad"; "I think that you have the power to make me feel good"; "I think you have the power to make me feel bad." Taibi Kahler, Ph.D., *Transactional Analysis Revisited*, Human Development Publications, Little Rock Arkansas, 1978.

27. PTM (*Process Therapy Model®*) sets out the defense mechanisms of the first degree of each type:

31 Workaholic: rationalization;
32 Persister: projection;
33 Harmonizer: internalization;
34 Rebel: transfer;
35 Dreamer: depersonalization;
36 Promoter: charm.

Taibi Kahler, Ph.D., *Transactional Analysis Script Profile (Guide for the Therapist)*, Taibi Kahler Associates, Inc., Little Rock, Arkansas, 1997.

28. PTM (*Process Therapy Model®*) presents the rackets, games and injunctions for each Personality Type, based on research and produced from a computer generated profile inventory. Taibi Kahler Ph.D., *The Transactional Analysis Script Profile*, Taibi Kahler Associates, Inc., Little Rock, Arkansas, 1997.

© March 1, 2006, Taibi Kahler, Ph.D.

ENDNOTES

i   Cited by P. Watzlawick, J. Beavin and D. Jackson, *Pragmatics of Human Communication: a study of interactional patterns, pathologies and paradoxes*, 1967

ii

iii   Watzlawick, Beavin and Jackson, *op. cit.*

Printed in Great Britain
by Amazon